Wanderlust Quilts

10 MODERN PROJECTS INSPIRED BY CLASSIC ART & ARCHITECTURE

Amanda Leins

stashBOOKS.
an imprint of C&T Publishing

PUBLISHER: Amy Marson

CREATIVE DIRECTOR: Gailen Runge

ART DIRECTOR / BOOK DESIGNER:
Kristy Zacharias

EDITOR: Lynn Koolish

TECHNICAL EDITORS: Priscilla Read and
Amanda Siegfried

PRODUCTION COORDINATOR:
Freesia Pearson Blizard

PRODUCTION EDITOR: Joanna Burgarino

ILLUSTRATOR: Valyrie Gillum

PHOTO ASSISTANT: Mary Peyton Peppo

STYLE PHOTOGRAPHY by Nissa Brehmer
and INSTRUCTIONAL PHOTOGRAPHY by
Diane Pedersen, unless otherwise noted

Published by Stash Books, an imprint of C&T Publishing, Inc., P.O. Box 1456,
Lafayette, CA 94549

Library of Congress Cataloging-in-Publication Data

Leins, Amanda, 1976-

Wanderlust quilts : 10 modern projects inspired by classic art & architecture / Amanda
Leins.

pages cm

Includes bibliographical references.

ISBN 978-1-61745-059-4 (soft cover)

1. Patchwork quilts. 2. Patchwork--Patterns. 3. Quilting--Patterns. I. Title.

TT835.L4255 2015

746.46--dc23

2014050235

Printed in China

10 9 8 7 6 5 4 3 2 1

PHOTOGRAPHY on pages 6, 9, 15, 23, 31, 43, 53,
and 63 courtesy of PhotoSpin.com

Contents

Dedication

Perfer et obdura; dolor hic tibi proderit olim.

Be patient and tough; someday this pain will be useful to you.

- Ovid -

To my best beloved, Ben, who first said,
"Have you ever thought of a longarm?"

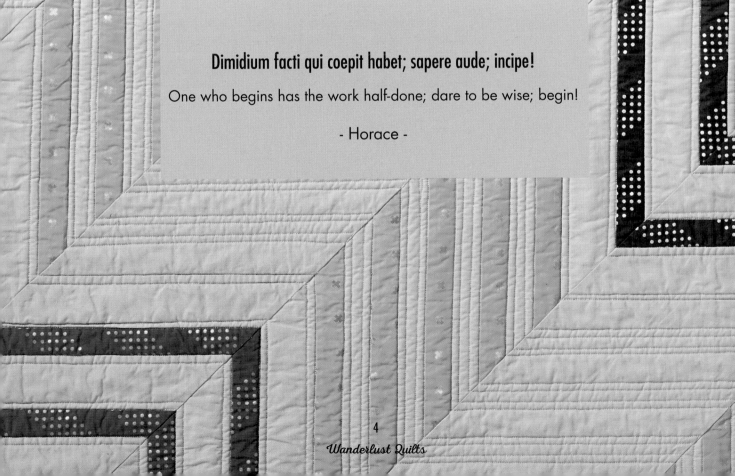

Dimidium facti qui coepit habet; sapere aude; incipe!

One who begins has the work half-done; dare to be wise; begin!

- Horace -

With Heartfelt Thanks

This journey of mine has been influenced by so many special people over the course of many years.

Thanks to my grandparents, Grampa Johnny and Gramma Nita, who started me on this journey, and my Grampa Townzen, who shared his Depression-era quilts that he had helped make as a six-year-old.

Thank you to my parents, Doug and Sylvia, who provided encouragement, even when I said, "You know, I think I want to be an archaeologist." They may have flinched, but they let me figure things out for myself, even when I said, "You know, I think I could give this quilt thing a go."

To my group of friends, the Memory Makers: Kathie, Cindy, Jo, Sally, Ann, Janet, Barb, Connie, Caryn, and Karen (who is always in our hearts), who provided decades of quilting and art experience—not to mention that it's nice to have a maternal group when my own mom lives so far away. Love you, ladies.

To the Mod Q Improv B group: Carolyn Hudson, Ronnie Haley, Cindy Russell, Teresa Pierce, Tina Michalik, Gretchen Kramer, Amanda Bennett, Myrth McDonald, Erin Stewart, Samantha Russell, Lauren Hungler, Rene Seltzer, and Adrienne Klenck, for inspiration, support, and generous gifts of made fabric.

To my friend Angela Walters, who first suggested I write that article and then that I should write that book proposal, and who encouraged me along the way to make this business of mine happen.

To my friend Cristy Fincher, for helping me refine my goals as a quilter and talking Big Quilty Ideas.

To my friend Serena Savage of Serena Savage Designs, for helping me with the digitization of the Pantheon for my *Architectural Sketch* quilt.

To my friends Melissa Averinos, Maddie Kertay, Ebony Love, and Molly Hanson, for being there and providing laughter, humor, perspective, and motivational kicks in the ass.

To my friend Kristi Ryan, for her help in piecing and quilting *Aqueducts* for me.

To my longarm quilter friends Penny Barnes and Liz Haskell, who helped me out and provided quilting for my biggest projects and who are a never-ending source of friendship, support, and encouragement.

To the lovely, amazing, and indispensable Susan Bishop, for her piecing, appliqué, and quilting skills; her enthusiasm; her support; and her general all-around awesomeness. I couldn't have done this without you, my friend.

I also couldn't have written this book without the help of Art Gallery Fabrics, Robert Kaufman Fabrics, Cotton + Steel (a division of RJR Fabrics), Cherrywood, and Studio E, which provided the beautiful fabrics, and Quilter's Dream batting, which provided a variety of battings

But most importantly, I want to thank my best beloved, Ben Lowery, for everything simple yet profound, and our kids, Jack and Lucy, for just being themselves. You're all my favorites.

Introduction

The quilts in this book are a material record of my personal journey as a quilter and a person—they tell the story of my past and my present and also point to where I hope to go. They tell of my loves and passions and show my quilting journey. What's more, I believe that every quilt goes on to have a life and story of its own, separate and independent from its maker. With this book, I am releasing my quilts into the wild, hoping that they carry with them some of the goals I had in making them:

• To show that modern quilts can be made using complex blocks and traditional techniques.

• To demonstrate that people of all ages speak the same language of pattern based on the natural world around us. Traditional quilt patterns are centuries and eons old and are a part of our shared human experience.

• To share some of the art, architecture, and history of ancient civilizations and the objects made by human hands that remain behind—to gain a fuller understanding of the people who lived in that time and place.

• To encourage quilters to grow in their craft, tempting them to try new skills and techniques.

Of all these goals, the last is the most important. I hope these quilts inspire you to try something new—to perhaps push yourself beyond your comfort zone. Use the methods and designs to expand your repertoire of techniques and to grow as a quilter. Some of the quilts are improvisational and free-form, and some are more technical and controlled, but I believe there is something for everyone, traditional or modern, experienced or beginner. Take your time and enjoy the process. Happy quilting!

My first experience with excavation was here at the remains of a Roman aqueduct on the coast of Israel, just outside Caesarea Maritima.

A Quick Note on Using the Patterns

Two of the projects in this book use patterns that are on a pullout pattern sheet at the back of the book and need to be traced. A lightbox is ideal for this, but a window will work as well.

1. Remove the pattern sheet from the back of the book. Smooth it out and place it over a lightbox or window.

2. Tape down the top edges of the pattern sheet with blue painter's tape (the kind that removes more easily from paper). Smooth out the paper so that it is perfectly flat and tape down the bottom edges of the pattern page.

3. Place the paper, foundation, or fusible web over the pattern, checking to see that it covers the entire area you need to trace. Tape it down around the outer edges.

4. Trace the pattern onto your paper, foundation, or fusible web.

Eggs and Darts

MADE BY Sue Bishop; quilted by Amanda Leins

FABRIC USED: Solids from the Pure Elements collection from Art Gallery Fabrics (Color names are shown in parentheses in Materials, page 10.)

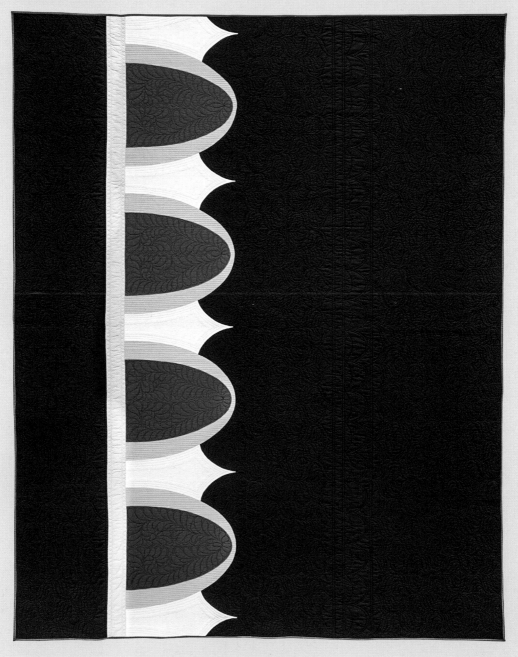

USING ARCHITECTURAL DETAILS

Scale, proportion, balance, harmony—these design principles have a very long history. Much of what we know of ancient architecture and design comes from Vitruvius' writings, *De Architectura*. Consisting of ten books, *De Architectura* discusses a wide range of topics related to architecture, civil engineering, and more.

De Architectura was "rediscovered" and translated into Italian and deeply influenced the great artists and architects of the Renaissance, including Leonardo da Vinci, who drew his own Vitruvian Man based on the concepts of proportion developed by Vitruvius. Even today, Vitruvian principles inform many design disciplines.

Why know these things? Chances are, you've come across a quilt that made you think, "Wow, that really works." Or…perhaps it didn't. Our responses to what we see often come from an intuitive understanding of when something is in proportion and balanced (or not). Vitruvius and others even had a word for it: *eurhythmia*, meaning harmonious and graceful. Being able to define what it is that makes us stop and pay attention means that we can better design quilts that suit our desires.

Bold in color and striking in size, the egg and dart motif was historically used as a very small detail on a temple, or as a bit of a border between features. It is a design element that often gets overlooked. By blowing up this detail to such a large size, I am employing a convention of modern art: playing with the scale of objects to create visual impact.

Don't be too surprised by the color choices for this quilt, though; they are deliberately bright. Archaeological evidence tells us that the ancient Greeks painted their temples bright greens, reds, yellows, and blues, sometimes even using bits of glass to add sparkle in the sunlight. As seen today, the Parthenon may seem spare and elegant, but it would have looked very different in the 5th century B.C.

Worn detail of the facade of the Pantheon, showing a teeny tiny egg and dart row

Materials

Note: The eggs and darts are appliquéd onto the dark background fabric. I used a stiff wash-away foundation paper and turned under the edges, following Sharon Schamber's technique. Another approach is to use paper-backed fusible web for raw-edge appliqué.

- FUCHSIA (CHERRY LIP GLOSS): 1 yard for eggs (Pattern A)
- YELLOW (EMPIRE YELLOW): 1 yard for egg echo (Pattern B)
- WHITE (LINEN WHITE): ¾ yard for dart (Pattern C)
- LIGHT MINT GREEN (SWEET MINT): ¼ yard for sashing
- DARK BLUE (NOCTURNAL): 3¾ yards for background
- BACKING: 4¾ yards
- BATTING: 70″ × 86″
- BINDING: ¾ yard (for 2½″ binding strips)

Other supplies

- WASH-AWAY FOUNDATION PAPER such as Wash-Away Appliqué Roll (fusible) or Sharon's Secret Foundation (see Resources, page 110): 1 package for turned-edge appliqué
  <u>OR</u>
- PAPER-BACKED FUSIBLE WEB: 2⅓ yards for raw-edge appliqué
- GLUE STICK for turned-edge appliqué
- CHALK OR HERA MARKER for marking

Cutting

The patterns are on the pattern pullout (page P2). You will need Pattern A, Pattern B, and Pattern C. You will need to cut the fabrics differently depending on which appliqué method you use. If you are using turned-edge appliqué, add your preferred seam allowance!

| WOF=width of fabric |

MAGENTA
Cut 4 using Pattern A.

YELLOW
Cut 4 using Pattern B.

WHITE
Cut 5 using Pattern C.

LIGHT MINT GREEN
Cut 3 strips 2½″ × WOF.

DARK BLUE
Cut 1 rectangle 40″ × 85″; from the remaining fabric, cut 4 rectangles 12½″ × 21¾″.

BINDING
Cut 8 strips 2½″ × WOF.

The egg and dart motif was historically used as a very small detail on a temple, or as a bit of a border between features.

CONSTRUCTION

Preparing for Turned-Edge Appliqué

The edges of the appliqué that are on top need to be turned under (refer to the notes on the printed patterns). An easy way to do this is to use a stiff wash-away foundation paper.

1. Cut foundations for Patterns A, B, and C.

2. Fuse or pin the foundations to the wrong side of the fabric. Cut the fabric, adding at least ¼″ around the edges where indicated on the printed pattern. Turn the seam allowances over the edges of the stiff foundation.

NOTE: Pattern A will overlap Pattern B by ¼″, so the top edge of Pattern B does not need to be folded over.

3. Carefully tack down the fabric to the foundation in these areas using a glue stick. Clip the seams on the concave sections of the appliqué (the "mouth of the cave" side—see Tip, page 19) as often as necessary to avoid puckers and points along the edge.

Preparing for Raw-Edge Appliqué

If you prefer to do raw-edge appliqué, I suggest you trace the patterns onto the paper side of the fusible web. Cut out the centers of the fusible web, leaving about 1½″ around the edge so the edges will be firmly attached to the quilt but the quilt will not be too stiff. Fuse the web to the fabric and cut the fabric along your traced pattern lines.

Tip

Before sewing on your quilt top, it's a good idea to sew a test on a sample prepared with the same appliqué method to make sure the stitch length and width and the tension are set correctly. For my quilt, I used the turned-edge preparation method and set my zigzag stitch to .9 stitch width and .9 stitch length. If you use invisible polyester thread, be advised that you will have to decrease your tension. For raw-edge appliqué, use a zigzag stitch or the stitch of your choice.

Remember that each machine is different. Do as many tests as needed to make sure your stitches are smooth and the fabric unpuckered.

Placing and Sewing the Appliqués

1. Place the dark blue 40″ × 85″ background rectangle on a large table or the floor. Using chalk or a Hera marking tool, mark a line 6″ from a long edge.

2. Using a square gridded ruler, mark lines 3½″ from the top and 3½″ from the bottom, perpendicular to the previous line.

3. Using 1 of these 2 lines as your starting point, mark lines every 9¾″.

4. Place the darts on the background, as shown in the diagram, by lining up the point of each dart where every other vertical and horizontal lines meet. Appliqué the darts to the background, sewing close to the turned-under or raw edges.

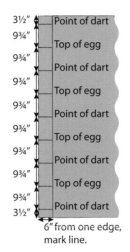

3½″ — Point of dart
9¾″ — Top of egg
9¾″ — Point of dart
9¾″ — Top of egg
9¾″ — Point of dart
9¾″ — Top of egg
9¾″ — Point of dart
9¾″ — Top of egg
9¾″ — Point of dart
3½″ — Point of dart

6″ from one edge, mark line.

5. Appliqué Pattern A to Pattern B to create 4 egg units.

6. Place the egg units on the background by lining up the center of the curved edge at the point where the vertical and horizontal lines meet. Appliqué the egg units onto the background and darts, sewing close to the turned-under or raw edges.

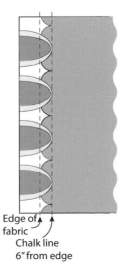

Edge of fabric
Chalk line 6″ from edge

Constructing the Top

Seam allowances are ¼″.

1. Piece together the light mint strips, short ends to short ends. Press the seams to one side. Cut a rectangle 2½″ × 85″.

2. Sew the rectangle to the left of the appliquéd eggs and darts. Press the seam to the mint strip to reduce bulk under the appliqué.

3. Sew together the 4 dark blue 12½″ × 21¾″ rectangles to make a rectangle 12½″ × 85½″. Press the seams toward the dark fabric.

4. Sew the 12½″ × 85″ rectangle to the light mint rectangle. Press the seams to 1 side.

Finishing

1. Layer the quilt top, batting, and backing and baste together the layers.

2. Quilt and then square up the quilt as needed. On my finished quilt, I trimmed the length to 78″, so the top and bottom darts are only partial.

3. Bind.

Aqueducts

MADE BY Kristi Ryan | **FABRIC USED:** made fabric provided by members of Mod Q Improv B

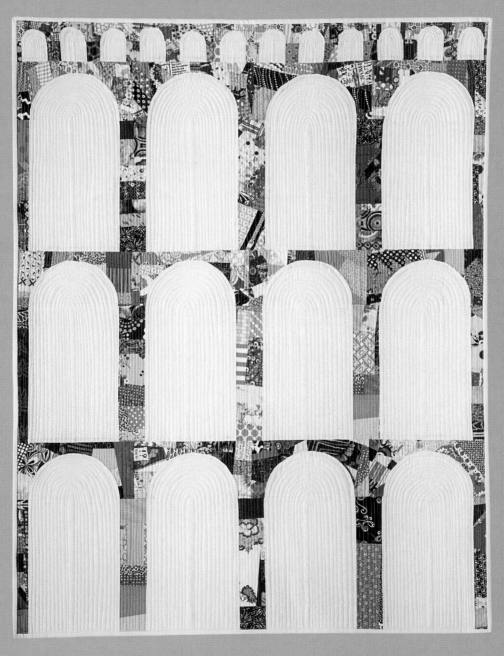

Aqueducts from across the Mediterranean; the Coliseum

In the ancient world, Roman aqueducts crossed great swathes of territory to provide the water that was vital to the survival of the empire and its people.

For centuries after the fall of the Roman Empire, these engineering marvels continued to supply fresh water to a multitude of people across the Mediterranean.

The piers and arches are a testament to the cleverness of the engineers, the extent of the aqueduct system is a testament to ambition and demand, and the aqueducts' maintenance through the centuries is a testament to pride and necessity.

In my own life, these aqueducts have become a sort of metaphor for the quilting world I find myself in: my quilty friends and family are from everywhere and love all types of quilting and are my solid supports. Between us all, we've built these amazing conduits of information that cross boundaries of traditional and modern and our love of the art and craft of quilting flows easily—that's where the inspiration for *Aqueducts* comes from. In particular, it shows the support and love of quilting from the members of my Mod Q Improv B improv group, who helped provide the awesome variety of fabric. Thanks, gals!

Materials

- **MADE-FABRIC:** Approximately 2 yards total, in sections large enough to cut the required pieces (see Made-Fabric, at right)
- **QUILTER'S LINEN:** 2½ yards
- **BACKING:** 1½ yards (using 44″-wide fabric)
- **BATTING:** 44″ × 54″
- **BINDING:** ½ yard (for 2½″ binding strips)

Cutting

Patterns are on the pattern pullout (page P2). You will need Patterns E, F, G, and H.

WOF=width of fabric

MADE-FABRIC

Cut 2 strips 1″ × 2″.

Cut 11 strips 1½″ × 2″.

Cut 6 strips 1½″ × 10½″.

Cut 9 strips 2½″ × 10½″.

Cut 12 using Pattern E and 12 using Pattern F. Note: It may be better to use made fabric that has bigger patches (and thus fewer seams) for the smaller arches.

QUILTER'S LINEN

Cut 3 strips 10½″ × WOF; subcut 12 rectangles 7½″ × 10½″ and 12 rectangles 2½″ × 10½″.

Cut 12 rectangles 2″ × 2½″.

Cut 12 using Pattern G and 12 using Pattern H.

BINDING

Cut 5 strips 2½″ × WOF.

Made-Fabric

I was happy to see Victoria Findlay Wolfe's work with *made-fabric* in *15 Minutes of Play*, a technique my great-grandmother used during the Depression when her scrap bag started to run out. Made-fabric is simply scraps of fabric sewn together with no plan in mind. While there are a number of ways to make made-fabric, here's how I often do it: Whenever I sew, I usually start off each seam with leader fabric for a nice, neat beginning, so I have a pile of scraps next to my sewing machine that I use as leaders and just keep sewing them together as I work on other projects. I press these leader pieces at the same time as the seams for the project I'm working on and then just keep adding to them as I work. When these bits get big enough, I join them together.

I like to have a lot of variety in my made-fabric, so I enlisted the help of friends who had different fabric collections. Having a swap with a group of friends is a fun and easy way to make sure your made-fabric is a riot of color.

Kristi Ryan made this quilt using the made-fabric for the aqueduct, but I think it would look equally striking with the made-fabric used as the background.

In my own life, these aqueducts have become a sort of metaphor for the quilting world I find myself in: My quilty friends and family are from everywhere and love all types of quilting and are my solid supports.

CONSTRUCTION

Seam allowances are ¼˝.

Aqueducts consists of 4 rows: 3 of the rows are composed of large arches (4 arch blocks per row) and the top row is made of the smallest arches, which act as a cap. Three mini arches fit over 1 large arch.

Sewing the Arches

Refer to Piecing Half-Circles (at right) and the quilt assembly diagram as needed.

1. Sew the large arch pieces (E) to the half-circle (G) pieces. Press the seams toward the half-circles.

2. Sew 4 arches together to make 3 rows. Press the seams whichever way makes them less bulky. This can vary depending on the way the seams of your made fabric fall.

3. Sew the small arch pieces (F) to the half-circle (H) pieces. Press the seams toward the half-circles.

4. Sew all the arches together to make a row. Press the seams whichever way makes them less bulky.

Piecing Half-Circles

NOTE: This technique also works for the quarter-circles in Drunkard's Path blocks.

1. Find the center of both the arch (concave curve) and the half-circle (convex curve) and mark them with either a light crease or another marking method. Find the halfway points between the center and the beginning and ending points and mark these as well. If you use a marking pen or pencil, keep the marks within the ¼˝ seam allowance.

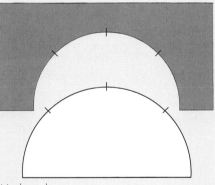

Marking the pieces

2. Place the 2 pieces right sides together as shown.

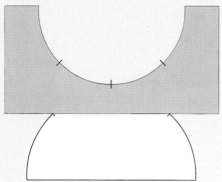

Line up the center point first, the outside edges second, and the interior marks third.

Tip

I use a somewhat silly mnemonic to remember that concave is the side that looks like the opening of the mouth of a cave.

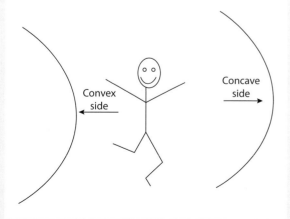

Convex side

Concave side

3. Line up all the marks and pin securely, including the base of the legs and circle. However, try to take only little nips of fabric with your pinning, so that you can ease the curves in as necessary.

4. Add pins ½″–1″ apart to help ease the fabric evenly around the curve and to secure it in place. Yes, it will be a little awkward to pin, but don't worry.

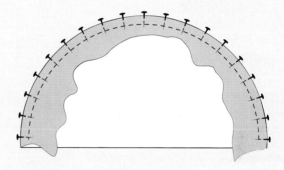

5. Sew the seam, beginning and ending with a few backstitches to secure it. Work carefully and as slowly as necessary to ensure that you aren't pulling or stretching the fabric.

6. When working with regular cotton fabric, clip the concave portion of the seam and press the seam toward the outside circumference of the circle. When working with made-fabric (page 16), you may find it is better to press the seam toward the circle, which will help reduce bulk.

Sewing the Large Columns

1. To make the end caps, sew 1 made-fabric 1½″ × 10½″ rectangle to 1 quilter's linen 7½″ × 10½″ rectangle. Make 6 end caps. The 1½″-wide made-fabric rectangles will always be on the ends, acting as caps for the rows. Press away from the quilter's linen.

Make 6 end caps.

2. Create 3 rows of columns by alternating the 3 made-fabric 2½″ × 10½″ rectangles with the 2 quilter's linen 7½″ × 10½″ rectangles. Always press away from the quilter's linen. Sew the end caps to the ends of each row.

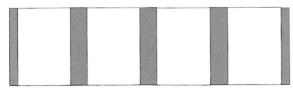

Make 3 rows.

3. Sew the rows of arches to the rows of columns, matching the seams as closely as possible. Because of the seams in the made-fabric, pressing the seams may be tricky, so do the best you can. Make 3 rows.

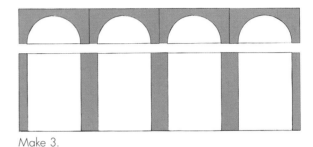

Make 3.

Sewing the Small Columns

1. To make the end caps, sew 1 made-fabric 1″ × 2″ rectangle to 1 quilter's linen 2″ × 2½″ rectangle. Press away from the quilter's linen. Make 2.

2. Create the row by alternating the made-fabric 1½″ × 2″ rectangles with the quilter's linen 2″ × 2½″ rectangles. Always press away from the quilter's linen. Sew an end cap to each end of the row.

3. Sew the row of arches to the row of rectangles, matching the seams as well as possible. Press whichever way works best with the bulkiness of the seams.

Finishing

1. Sew together the rows of arches.

2. Layer the quilt top, batting, and backing and baste together the layers.

3. Quilt and bind.

Quilt assembly

Architectural Sketch

MADE BY Amanda Leins | **FABRIC USED:** Cherrywood Hand Dyed Fabrics

The Pantheon in Rome has been in constant use since the time of Augustus.

It's not uncommon to hear the advice, "Take your sketchbook with you; you just never know what might inspire you."

This quilt is based on one of my sketches of the Pantheon in Rome. The building itself is an engineering marvel, with a beautiful dome built entirely out of cement. For such a pedestrian material, it's amazing that when you enter the space, it is filled with light and air and a sense of soaring openness, all guiding your eyes up and out. Beginning in the time of Hadrian (who rebuilt it in A.D. 125 after it was destroyed), it was used in various ways until it became a Roman Catholic church in the seventh century. When I was in Rome, I would often walk in and lean against a pillar and do a quick sketch to try to capture all the things I saw that inspired me.

I have included the pattern for you to make a wallhanging just like mine, but I encourage you to think about the places and spaces you've been to that have struck you. Refer to Turning Your Photos or Sketches into a Quilt (page 29) and think about using your own sketches and photos to recreate your own memories in fabric.

Materials

I chose hand dyes from Cherrywood bundles for my project because they were close to the soothing brown and gray neutrals I saw in the Pantheon and in the native tufa stone of Italy. To me, these fabrics evoked the look of the stone and cement when touched by the light. Likewise, I chose threads that recalled the colors of my original pencils and Conté crayons. Choosing fabrics and threads that appeal to you is a great way to branch out and experiment. You can use whatever you'd like!

- **QUILT TOP:** Assorted fabrics, approximately 1½ yards (I chose 5 values of the same color); for the large curves, you need 2 pieces each approximately 12″ × width of fabric

- **BACKING:** 1 yard

- **BATTING:** 31″ × 39″

- **BINDING:** ⅓ yard

Other supplies

- Various threads for accent quilting

- Sharpie fine-point permanent marker

- Fabric-marking pencils or regular colored pencils

- Lightbox or window for tracing pattern pieces

- Freezer paper to make templates

Cutting

WOF=width of fabric

The pattern for this quilt is on the pattern pullout (page P1) at the back of the book. To make templates from the pattern, refer to Making Freezer-Paper Templates for Piecing (page 26), which is based on Ruth McDowell's piecing technique (see Resources, page 110). If you have another preferred method, by all means use the method you are most comfortable with.

After you make the templates, decide how you want the colors to work together. The placement of the lights and darks creates different perspectives. I wanted my brighter fabrics toward the ceiling, where the light came in through the dome, and the darker fabrics toward the floor, where the shadows gathered. It may seem like a little detail, but it is one that makes a big difference when working to create a sense of shape and scale, and it's worth the time to figure out. Using Ruth's piecing method allows you to cut out and preview all your fabric choices before you start to sew.

This quilt is based on one of my sketches of the Pantheon in Rome.

25

Architectural Sketch

The following instructions are a brief how-to on using freezer paper to make piecing templates. I highly recommend *Ruth McDowell's Piecing Workshop*, available as a print-on-demand book from C&T Publishing. Ruth has refined this technique to a fine art, and her book shows you everything you need to know about piecing.

Making the Templates

1. Place the pattern on a lightbox or window.

2. Using masking tape on the paper side of the freezer paper, tape together pieces to make a piece at least 25˝ × 32˝.

3. Place the freezer paper *shiny side up* on top of the pattern.

4. Using a Sharpie permanent marker, trace over all the lines of the pattern, including the outside straight lines.

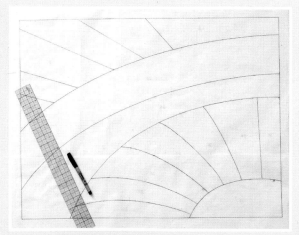

Pattern traced on the shiny side of the freezer paper

5. Remove the pattern sheet, turn over the freezer paper so the paper side is facing up, and trace all the lines from the shiny side using a pencil.

6. Referring to the original pattern, label all the pieces on the paper side of the freezer paper. Keep in mind that what you are labeling is the mirror image of the original pattern.

7. For each piece, make registration marks on the paper side to help you align the pieces when you sew them together.

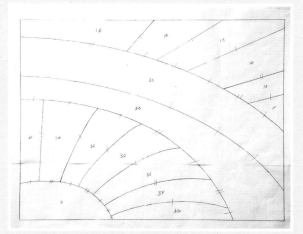

Paper side with pieces labeled and registration marks added

8. Cut apart the freezer paper on the lines and put all the pieces up on a design wall to keep them in order.

Cutting

1. As you decide which fabric to use for each piece, place the *shiny side* of the freezer paper on the *back side* of the fabric and press with a hot, dry iron to hold it in place (the shiny side of the freezer paper adheres to the fabric but is easy to remove).

2. Cut out each piece, adding a ¼″ seam allowance. Try to be consistent but don't worry about being exact because you will mark the sewing lines in the next step.

3. With a fabric marker or colored pencil, draw around all the edges of each piece. Transfer the registration marks into the seam allowances.

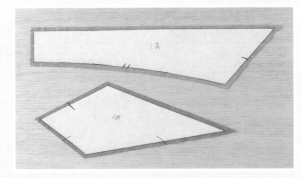

4. With the freezer paper still attached, put the pieces back up on the design wall, fabric side facing out.

Cut out and mark all the pieces and put them up on the design wall *before* you do any sewing. With this technique you can see all your fabric choices and make any changes before you sew a stitch.

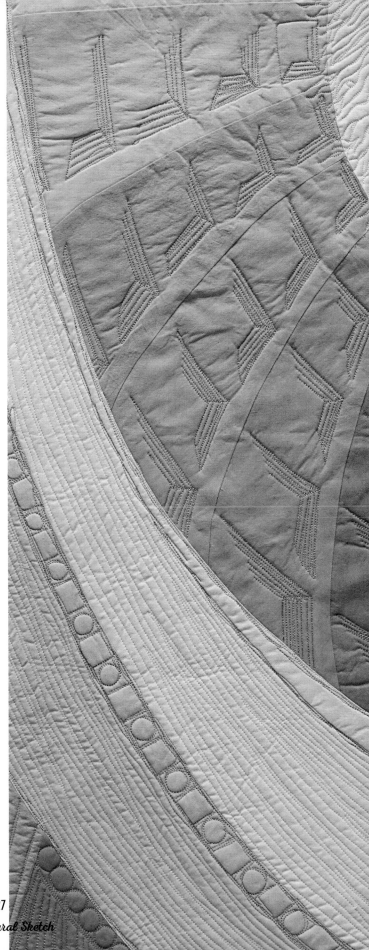

CONSTRUCTION

Making the Quilt Top

1. Sew together the pieces in Section 1 in numerical order. For example, sew 1A to 1B, then add 1C, and so on. Use the sewing lines and registration marks to line up the pieces correctly. Press the seam allowances toward the darker fabric.

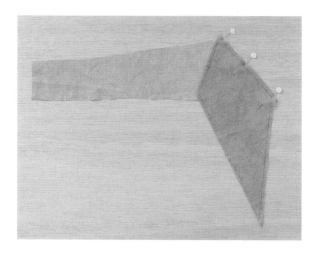

2. Continue sewing together the pieces for each section. When piecing the large curves for Sections 2, 3, and 4, use the registration marks to line up the edges of the pieces and evenly distribute the fabric between the registration marks (similar to piecing a circle), pinning the pieces in place. Press the seam allowances toward the darker fabric.

3. Sew Section 1 to Section 2, using the registration marks to line up the seams. Press the seam allowances toward Section 1.

4. Sew Section 3 to Section 4. Press the seam allowances toward Section 4.

5. Pin together Section 1-2 and Section 3-4, using the registration marks to line up the sections. Sew; then press the seams toward Section 1-2.

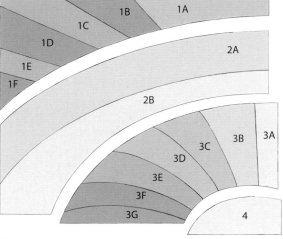

Quilt assembly

Finishing

1. Using a lightbox or window, place the pieced top back over the pattern, lining up the seamlines.

2. With either a washable marker or a chalk pencil, sketch in the areas for detailed quilting. *If you use a washable blue pen, do not iron or expose your quilt to heat until after it has been washed—otherwise those blue lines will be permanent!*

3. Layer the quilt top, batting, and backing and baste together the layers.

4. Quilt as desired. I chose a rough-sketch style of quilting to make it look like my drawings. Hand quilting with big stitches would look great as well. I recommend stitching in-the-ditch first to secure all the layers.

5. Square up the quilt as needed and bind.

Turning Your Photos or Sketches into a Quilt

If you don't have access to a program such as Adobe Illustrator or Photoshop for tracing and/or enlarging, you can still make your own pattern and templates from a photo or sketch, either by taking it to a copy shop to be enlarged or by using an enlarging technique that is thousands of years old.

To do your own enlarging:

1. If your photo or drawing is smaller than about 8″ × 10″, enlarge it first so the details are larger. Trace over the photo, drawing, or enlarged copy, establishing the seamlines that you will use for piecing. Think about how you can piece (or appliqué) the quilt top, keeping in mind that it is often best to use the larger shapes for piecing and the smaller details for quilting. **A**

2. Draw a 1″ × 1″ grid on a sheet of clear plastic from an office supply store. The exact size of the squares doesn't matter here, as long as your grid lines are perfectly square and evenly spaced. **B**

3. Decide how large you would like your finished project to be. On a large sheet of paper (or several sheets of paper taped together), draw a grid that has the exact same number of squares. The difference here, though, is that the squares must be large enough to fill up the space on the large sheet of paper. I like to use my largest gridded rulers and squares for this process.

4. Place the transparent grid over the image that has the seamlines. Square by square, look at your drawing and draw in the lines on the corresponding larger square. **C**

5. Create freezer-paper templates as described in Cutting (page 27) and you're well on your way to making your own work of art.

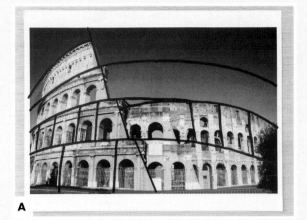

A

B

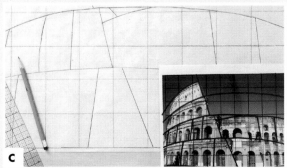

C

Flowing Fabric

MADE BY Amanda Leins

FABRIC USED: Kona Cotton Solids from Robert Kaufman Fabrics in Tomato, Lipstick, Rich Red, Cardinal, and Ruby, with Tangerine and Ice Frappe as accent colors

The caryatids form the columns of the Erechtheum, a temple dedicated to the goddess Athena and the god Poseidon, on the Acropolis in Athens.

When I think about my current fascination with fabrics and quilting, I can't help but laugh and shake my head. My love of all things textile was often thwarted studying classical archaeology because textiles had to have the exact right conditions to be preserved for such a great length of time.

Much of what little we do know about ancient textiles comes from vase paintings and sculpture and, sometimes, written descriptions.

This project is one of my favorites because it appeals to my sense of irony and humor: I'm re-creating, in cloth, how an ancient person's clothing looked based on representations on a vase.

In the ancient world, red dye (sometimes called Tyrian purple) was made from the tiny gland of a specific type of murex, and was jaw-droppingly expensive because it took thousands of these mollusks to make one ounce of dye. Draping the fabric across my lap, I feel a little decadent too. I chose to work in shades of red not only because I like the contrast of the reds, orange, and aqua, but because in ancient times it was a color reserved only for the elite or wealthy, and using it appeals to my sense of humor.

Materials

- **MAIN COLOR:** 2 yards of each color (choose shades that are close to each other but that still provide enough contrast to register as different to your eyes). I recommend getting 2 yards of each so that you can cut the pieces from the length of the fabric, but if you don't mind a straight seam across the middle you can easily use 2 half-yard pieces sewn together, short end to short end.

- **ONE COLOR THAT IS ANALOGOUS TO YOUR MAIN COLOR:**
  ½ yard for top accent

- **ONE COLOR THAT IS THE COMPLEMENT OF THE TOP ACCENT:**
  ¾ yard for bottom accent

- **BACKING, BATTING, AND BINDING:** Measure your quilt top once it is finished to determine how much you'll need.

- **WASHABLE MARKER OR CHALK PENCIL**

A Quick Color Lesson: Analogous, Complementary, and Split Complementary

Selecting fabric colors can sometimes be a challenge. If you want some help in this area, I highly recommend Joen Wolfrom's *Ultimate 3-in-1 Color Tool* (Resources, page 110). I knew I wanted the main color of this quilt to be red, so I selected five values of red. For the top curved accents I knew I wanted to use orange. Orange is next to red on the color wheel, so red and orange are analogous colors—colors that always work harmoniously together. For the bottom accent

curves, I wanted something that would provide a visual pop, so I went with a very light aqua green, which is across from orange on the color wheel, and thus is its complement.

This combination of analogous and complementary colors is known as a split-complementary color scheme. It has the visual punch of complementary colors but is moderated by the analogous colors.

Cutting

MAIN COLOR

1. Press the fabrics well. Sew together your main-color fabrics if you bought ½-yard pieces.

2. Place the fabric on a flat surface (probably the floor) large enough so that you have access to the entire surface of the fabric. Beginning at a short end at the left corner, cut a line at a shallow angle to the opposite side. Repeat, this time with the angle in the opposite direction. Your goal is to cut large wedges that taper gracefully. Each wedge should be between 6″ and 12″ at the base and between 2″ and 5″ at the top. I like to keep the wedges for each color roughly the same sizes. Cut the narrowest wedges from the lightest fabric and gradually increase the width of the wedges so that the widest wedges are cut from the darkest fabric. I used 4 wedges of the medium-value fabrics and 2 wedges of the lightest and darkest fabrics.

Tips

- It is quick and easy to stack all 5 fabrics and cut them together, but I like the variety of shape that comes from cutting each piece individually.

- You can cut the wedges freehand, but I like to use a laser level from the hardware store to help keep my cuts straight—this cuts down on time spent tweaking the seams to keep them flat. However you choose to cut, keep your cuts as straight as you can. Remember to include enough on the sides for a seam allowance.

3. Arrange the wedges, roughly following the diagram (at right). I started laying out the wedges from right to left and began with 3 of the medium values rather than a light or dark wedge. This quilt is meant to look like a circle skirt as it is draped across a lap, with a narrower "waist" at the top and a full "skirt" at the bottom, so it is important to build that into the pieced top from the beginning. Your layout will look different from this because of differences in cutting and personal preference, but in general there will be a narrower top and a wider bottom. **A**

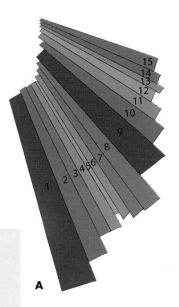

A

> ## Tip
>
> This is an excellent time to look at where your seams will be and maybe even pin them together along the ¼˝ seam to see if there will be anything to contend with once you start sewing, such as curved cuts that aren't immediately obvious. If you do notice these, try to correct them now by trimming or marking the points where you want the seams to be. When you're satisfied, mark each wedge with a chalk number, from left to right.

ACCENTS

NOTE: Before you begin cutting the accent pieces, look at the wedges and consider where you might trim the quilt top at the end. If you will be trimming to maintain the curved waist at the top and the full skirt at the bottom, this may change where you want the accent pieces to go.

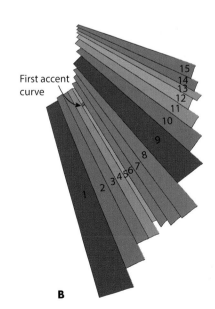

First accent curve

B

1. Identify the lightest-value fabric wedge. Use chalk or another fabric marker to mark the first accent curve about 10˝ from where a possible trimming line might be and about 2˝–3˝ wide. This curve will provide the beginning point for all the other curves. To highlight the way the light and dark fabrics provide highlights and shadows of folds, I place the uppermost highlight on the lightest fabric. **B**

Accent Tips

- Make sure you place the highest accents high enough that you don't run out of space for the lower accents.

- Remember that you will be losing some of the edge to seam allowances, so try to keep the deepest part of the curve toward the center so it won't be cut off.

- Decide how noticeable you want the accents to be. For the smaller set of curves, I used the orange, so as not to overwhelm the rest of the design at the top, and saved the aqua accents for the bottom, where they make a statement.

2. Working outward to the next wedges, sketch the next curves so they fall just below the first curves. The lowest curve will automatically be on the darkest fabric. Be sure to label each curve with the number of its wedge. **C**

3. To mark the second set of accent curves, begin about 10˝ up from the bottom of the leftmost dark wedge (1 on the diagram) and mark the accent curves. I like to make this set of curves wider, usually 4˝–5˝. Working outward to the next wedges, sketch them in so they are *just* above the first lower sketched curve.

4. Continue marking the second set of curves. Be sure to label each curve with the number of its wedge. **D**

5. Cut out the accent curves along the marked lines.

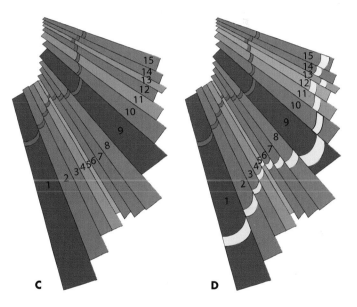

C

D

USING THE CUT-OUT ACCENT CURVES AS TEMPLATES

1. Place the cut-out upper accent curves right side up (the side with the chalk numbers) on top of your chosen analogous fabric color, leaving about 1″ of space around them.

2. Using a pencil or fine-point marking tool, trace around the exact shape and then add a ¼″ seam allowance to the top and bottom edges. Be sure to keep the curve the same! Do this for all the accent pieces, upper and lower.

3. Cut out each accent piece along the new lines and stack it with its red fabric wedge.

Tracing Tips

To make the tracing easier, try the following:

- Put a sandpaper board, or just a plain piece of fine-grit sandpaper, underneath the fabric—the grit will hold onto the fabric, making it easier to draw on.

- If you have a dressmaker's sewing gauge, set it to ¼″ and use it to add the ¼″ seam allowance.

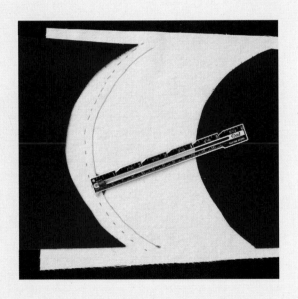

I'm re-creating, in cloth, how an ancient person's clothing looked based on representations on a vase.

CONSTRUCTION

Seam allowances are ¼˝.

Sewing Together the Wedges

1. Sew each curved accent piece into its correct space using the same technique as for half-circles (page 18). Press the seams toward the bottom edge of the quilt top.

2. Arrange all the wedges and line them up so that the accent curves fall as you planned them. As you sew the wedges together, check each seam for cupping or waviness and adjust the seams as necessary.

3. Trim the seams to ¼˝ if necessary and press the seam allowances to one side.

Finishing

1. Layer the quilt top, batting, and backing and baste together the layers.

2. Quilt.

3. Trim the top into a shape that is pleasing to you. This could be a rectangular shape, but I prefer to cut the top to mimic the full, swinging skirts of a robed figure—it looks really great when you're using it as a lap quilt.

Sketch out your planned cutting line in chalk to make sure you're satisfied before you cut. If you are cutting curved corners, make sure they are smooth and not too narrow, or they will be difficult to bind.

4. Bind (see Binding a Quilt with Scalloped Edges, page 39).

Tip

I prefer to quilt an improv top such as this *before* I trim it to the finished shape. This has two benefits:

- It allows me to manipulate the fabric in any way necessary if there are any waves or bumps.

- I can more easily visualize where I want to trim.

If you choose to quilt first, though, make sure that your quilting stitches are short enough not to pull out after you sew the binding on. You can sew the binding on with smaller stitches to trap those cut threads or staystitch ⅛˝ from the cut edge.

Binding a Quilt with Scalloped Edges

Any quilt that has curved or scalloped edges should be bound with binding cut on the bias (See Making Continuous Bias Binding, page 40). The added stretch allows you to manipulate the binding more easily as you go around those curves.

Because the quilts in the book that need bias-cut binding are improvisational, the curves vary in size and shape. The directions below take that into account and differ slightly from instructions for traditional scalloped binding.

1. Begin sewing the binding to the quilt as usual, leaving a length of binding tail. If you are working on a quilt with both curved and straight edges, start on a straight edge.

Tip

If you are binding curves with binding made from bias strips, it can be very easy to stretch out the binding by accident. I recommend that you take your time and sew the binding on slowly, being careful to ease the binding in so that it is not stretched in any way. It will look a little ripply as you ease it in, but that's okay—the fabric needs to be able to go all the way over the edge of the curve. You can use clips to hold it in place, but I prefer to have the binding free for me to maneuver under the sewing machine needle.

2. About 3″ before you reach an interior corner, mark the ¼″ seam allowances before and after the interior corner. Place a pin or mark an X using a washable marker or chalk pencil where the seam allowances will cross over. Carefully clip the corner to just within the seam allowance.

If you use a washable blue pen, do not iron or expose your quilt to heat until after it has been washed— otherwise those blue lines will be permanent!

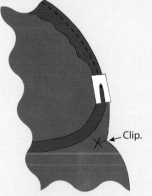

Clip just inside the seam allowance.

3. Continue sewing the binding along the edge, stopping at the mark you made in Step 2 *with the needle down.*

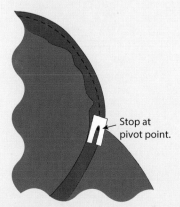

Stop with the needle down where the lines cross.

4. Working carefully so as not to tear the clipped corner, pull on the bottom edge so that the corner and following curve become nearly straight.

5. Hold the straightened edge firmly in place. Straighten the binding, trying not to distort it, and continue to sew the binding on with a ¼″ seam allowance—making sure the stitching is outside the clipped area. Release your hold and readjust the top about ½″ from the point of the interior corner. Continue as before and join the ends of the binding. **A**

A

6. Fold the binding to the back of the quilt and stitch it down by hand. At each of the interior corners, the binding should fold over itself slightly to make a neat crease. Stitch the crease down as well.

Making Continuous Bias Binding

Continuous bias involves slicing a square in half diagonally and then sewing the triangles together so that you can cut marked strips to make continuous bias binding.

Determine the size of square you'll need as follows: Measure the perimeter (outside edges) of your quilt. Multiply this by the width of the strips you'll be cutting. Take the square root of the number to determine the size of square you'll need. Example: For my quilt, 2¼″ strips × 284″ around quilt = 639. The square root of 639 is 25.278, so I started with a 26″ square.

The same instructions can be used to cut bias for piping. Cut the fabric for the bias binding or piping so it is a square. Cut the square in half diagonally, creating 2 triangles.

Sew these triangles together as shown, using a ¼″ seam allowance. Press the seam open. **B**

Using a ruler, mark the parallelogram created by the 2 triangles with lines spaced the width you need to cut the bias. Cut about 5″ along the first line. **C**

Join Side 1 and Side 2 to form a tube. The raw edge at point A will align with the raw edge at B. This will allow the first line to be offset by 1 strip width. Pin the raw edges right sides together, making sure that the drawn lines match. Sew with a ¼″ seam allowance. Press the seam open. Cut along the drawn lines, creating a continuous strip. **D**

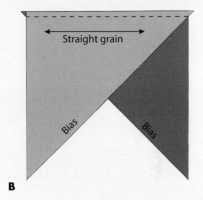

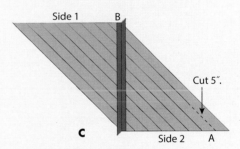

Going Places

MADE BY Amanda Leins | **FABRIC USED:** Cherrywood Hand Dyed Fabrics

With so much to see in the historic cities of Europe, it's really hard not to look like a tourist all the time; even looking down proves distracting, with the roughly squared cobbles beneath your feet telling their own stories.

Often using basalt, the hardest of the volcanic stones, or a lighter and softer stone known as tufa, pavement construction in Italy has remained more or less consistent over thousands of years: flatten out the space for your road, lay out your cobbles, fill in between the cobbles with sand.

One pattern of cobbles, in particular, has always stood out to me—as a quilter, I look at it and think of clamshells. This clamshell pattern was a common one in the ancient world, particularly in Roman mosaic floors, and makes for a fun improv quilt. While I worked on this, I thought of laying foundations with my stitches and telling a story with my fabric choices. I decided that this would be a baby quilt, the beginning of the road for some little person. The lighter colors are reminiscent of tufa, and the darker colors are for basalt. The variety of colors between the stones reminds me of the rainbows you see on pavement after rain.

Materials

- **COBBLES**: 2½–3 yards total of various gray and black fabrics in a range of values (I used a Cherrywood half-yard bundle and a few additional pieces.)

- **SAND FILLER**: Assorted scraps totaling about 1 yard (The scraps will be cut into strips and should be a minimum of 1½″ wide. Include brightly colored fabric and more subdued neutral colors.)

- **BATTING**: Variable, depending on finished size of quilt

- **BACKING**: Variable, depending on finished size of quilt

- **BINDING**: ½ yard (You may need more fabric if your quilt is larger than the one shown.)

Cutting

COBBLES

I cut a variety of sizes of cobbles and grouped those of similar size together. My cobbles varied in size from around 4″ to 6″. Each of the cobbles was either squarish or slightly tapered, sometimes on one side, sometimes on two.

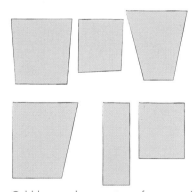

Cobbles can be a variety of trapezoid shapes.

Stack the black and gray fabrics together, up to 4 at a time, and cut the shapes using a rotary cutter. It may be easier to cut strips the width you want and then cut the trapezoids from these, alternating angles as shown to get the most from your fabric.

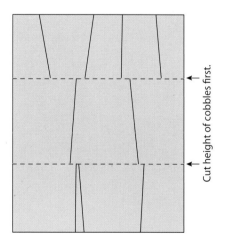

Cut height of cobbles first.

SAND FILLER

Cut strips from the colorful scraps approximately 1½″–2″ wide. You'll be piecing the strips together, so if you want more variety, make the strips short, and if you want less variety, make the strips longer. I grouped mine according to value because I wanted the lighter values to be with the lighter gray cobbles and the more saturated, brighter values to be with the darker grays and blacks.

CONSTRUCTION

Making the Sand Filler

Piece together the strips to make long multicolored strips. Press the seams to one side. I sewed some strips with a straight vertical seam and some on an angle. I mostly kept the light and dark values separated.

Making the Cobbles

My quilt top is composed of 2 kinds of blocks (or cobbles). A blocks have columns and caps. B blocks just have caps.

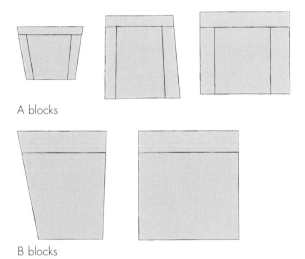

A blocks

B blocks

The A and B blocks alternate across each row, with the narrower points of the trapezoids at the base; the wide parts are at the top. When you piece the blocks together, this will automatically make an arc shape.

Tip

You will need quite a bit of this strip filler. I recommend making somewhere in the neighborhood of 20–30 yards. It may seem tedious to do all at once, but it is much more satisfying than having to hop up and make more every 5 minutes!

Tip

Before you begin, divide your stacks of cobbles into value groups that you like. I made a light group and a dark group, and a small group of medium values to mix in. While it is possible to arrange the fans before you begin piecing, I like the truly random aspect of piecing everything together and then laying it out. Despite being a real control freak in some ways, I find it very freeing to relax and see what happens.

Making the A Blocks

1. Divide your dark value group about in half. Using half of the dark group and the long, colorful strip, start chain piecing the cobbles to the edge of the strip, skipping about 1˝ between cobbles.

2. Continue until all the cobbles in that group have been sewn onto the strip. At the end, cut off the strip.

3. Now sew the opposite sides of the same cobbles to the strip you just cut off, using the same method, so you have colorful strips on both sides of the cobbles.

4. Press the seams toward the cobbles and cut apart the cobbles.

5. In the same manner, sew the *tops* of the A blocks to the strip.

6. Press the seams toward the cobbles and cut each A block from the strip.

A block. Press the seam to the cobble.

Making the B Blocks

1. Sew the tops of the remaining cobbles to the strip as you did for the A blocks (at left).

2. Press the seams toward the top and cut each B block from the strip.

B block. Press the seam to the top.

I decided that this would be a baby quilt, the beginning of the road for some little person.

Making the Quilt Top

Making Clamshell 1

1. Using a design wall or space on the floor, start laying out the first row of cobbles, which will provide the base for the other rows in the clamshell. Begin with 3 or 4 blocks, alternating A and B blocks. Next, lay out the second row. You should notice the beginning of an arc, which will become more pronounced with subsequent rows. Continue laying out rows, building up and out, until you have laid out a shape that is more or less the shape of a clamshell.

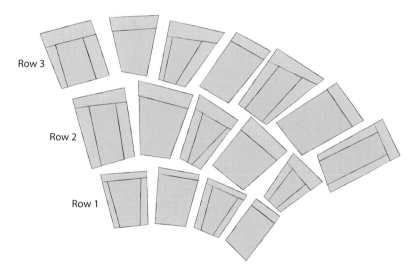

2. Beginning with the bottom row, piece together the A and B blocks, pressing the seam allowances toward the B blocks. Piece together all the rows for the clamshell.

> ## *Tip*
>
> If any of the cobbles are not angled enough to make a deep enough curve, sew the seam where you want it to be. Then trim off any excess. Create the shape you want, working row by row until all the rows in the clamshell are done.

3. The row at the bottom is Row 1. Place Row 1 on top of Row 2 as you would like it to be positioned, making sure that Row 1 covers the bottom edge of Row 2. It is okay if there is major overlap of the second row.

4. Using the top of the first row as your guide, make a cut through both layers, following the curve of the first row to create matching curves.

5. Make small registration marks so you can line up the curved edges when you sew them together.

6. Place the rows right sides together, lining up the registration marks—you may want pin at these points. Sew with the concave curve on the top.

7. Open up the seam and check to see if there are any spots that are too full, creating a "bubble" effect where you need to redistribute the fullness. It is much easier to rip out a few stitches and readjust your seams as necessary at this point, rather than waiting to deal with any problems at the end. Sometimes adding more pieced sand filler into the opened seam is a good option.

8. After making any adjustments, trim the excess fabric from the seam and press it toward the second row.

9. Repeat with the remaining rows of the first clamshell.

Making Clamshells 2–4

1. Starting with B blocks, begin each row where the blocks butt against Clamshell 1, building the rows out and to the right. The length and number of the rows depends on how big you want the quilt to be. You want to add enough rows to reach about halfway up the side of the first shell.

2. Sew together the rows to make the second clamshell. Make sure this section has a curve similar to the top of Clamshell 1 where it will butt up.

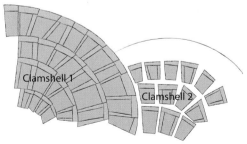

The first clamshell is used as the base for the remaining shells.

3. Clamshell 3 follows the top curve of Clamshell 1, with the cobbles oriented the same direction. This time, begin building with B blocks from the *top edge* of Clamshell 2. Sew together the rows as before. Notice that you now have clamshells that mimic the curve of Clamshell 1.

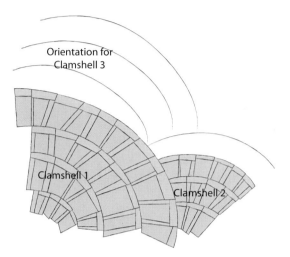

4. Clamshell 4 fills in the gap between Clamshells 2 and 3, with the cobbles oriented in the same direction as those in Clamshell 2. Make this last clamshell in the same way as the previous ones.

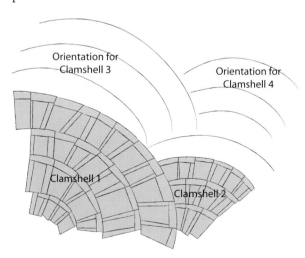

5. Using the same cutting technique as when joining rows, layer Clamshell 3 over Clamshell 4 and cut a matching curve through both layers at once. Sew together the clamshells as if you were sewing rows.

6. Layer Clamshell 2 over Clamshell 3-4 and cut a matching curve. Sew together the clamshells as before.

7. Layer Clamshell 1 over Clamshell 2-3-4 and cut a matching curve through both layers at once. Sew together the sections as before.

Finishing

1. Layer the quilt top, batting, and backing and baste together the layers.

Tip

I prefer to quilt before cutting the final shape. This gives me the fabric needed to ease in any waviness and puffs in the top itself and allows me to get the largest quilt possible.

2. Quilt and bind (see Binding a Quilt with Scalloped Edges, page 39).

Layered Conversations

PIECED BY Amanda Leins and Susan Bishop; quilted by Penny Barnes

FABRIC USED: Kona Cotton Solids from Robert Kaufman Fabrics

Looking across the Roman Forum, with buildings of every age within one view

My first time as an American traveling abroad, I was a wide-eyed and slightly nervous undergrad off to practice archaeology on the coast of Israel. I was constantly struck by how young a country the United States really is. Jerusalem, Rome, Athens…these ancient cities are still standing and thriving, their histories leaving a lasting impression on their people.

With ancient and modern structures all jumbled together, it's hard to ignore how the present is built on the past.

Layered Conversations was inspired by these ideas.

Materials

- GRAY: 7 yards
- GREEN 1 (LIGHTEST): 1 fat quarter
- GREEN 2: 1 fat quarter
- GREEN 3: 1 fat quarter
- GREEN 4: 2 fat quarters
- GREEN 5 (DARKEST): 2 fat quarters

- PINK 1 (LIGHTEST): ½ yard
- PINK 2: ½ yard
- PINK 3: ⅝ yard
- PINK 4: ⅝ yard
- PINK 5 (DARKEST): ⅝ yard

- ORANGE: ⅝ yard (If you are absolutely certain your fabric will be at least 40½″ wide after all your prep for cutting is complete, you can get by with ⅜ yard.)
- BACKING: 9¾ yards
- BINDING: ⅞ yard
- BATTING: 112″ × 112″

Cutting

Tip

I suggest you label everything with its size, using a small piece of paper pinned through all the pieces to keep them together. Before you begin piecing, organize the pieces in size order, from smallest to largest. You may want to stack the strips and cut a few at a time.

WOF=width of fabric

GRAY BACKGROUND
Cut 54 strips 4½″ × WOF. Subcut:

- Each of 4 strips into 1 rectangle 4½″ × 18½″ and 1 rectangle 4½″ × 20½″ (total of 4 each).

- Each of 4 strips into 1 rectangle 4½″ × 16½″, 1 rectangle 4½″ × 14½″, and 1 rectangle 4½″ × 8½″ (total of 4 each).

- Each of 4 strips into 1 rectangle 4½″ × 12½″, 1 rectangle 4½″ × 10½″, and 1 rectangle 4½″ × 15½″ (total of 4 each).

- Each of 4 strips into 1 rectangle 4½″ × 22½″ and 1 rectangle 4½″ × 15½″ (total of 4 each).

- Each of 4 strips into 1 rectangle 4½″ × 39½″ (total of 4).

- Each of 8 strips into 1 rectangle 4½″ × 31½″ and 1 rectangle 4½″ × 7½″ (total of 8 each).

- Each of 8 strips into 1 rectangle 4½″ × 35½″ and 1 rectangle 4½″ × 3½″ (total of 8 each).

- Each of 8 strips into 1 rectangle 4½″ × 27½″ and 1 rectangle 4½″ × 19½″ (total of 8 each).

- Each of 8 strips into 1 rectangle 4½″ × 23½″ and 1 rectangle 4½″ × 11½″ (total of 8 each).

- 1 strip into 1 rectangle 4½″ × 6½″, 2 squares 4½″ × 4½″, and 6 rectangles 4½″ × 3½″. Select 4 of the 4½″ × 3½″ rectangles and cut them down to 3½″ × 3½″ squares.

- The remaining strip into 4 rectangles 4½″ × 6½″.

GREEN FABRIC 1

Cut 3 strips 1½″ × length of fat quarter. Subcut:

- 1 strip into 2 rectangles 1½″ × 4½″, 1 rectangle 1½″ × 3½″, and 1 rectangle 1½″ × 6½″.

- 1 strip into 2 rectangles 1½″ × 4½″ and 3 rectangles 1½″ × 3½″.

- 1 strip into 3 rectangles 1½″ × 6½″.

GREEN FABRIC 2

Cut 6 strips 1½″ × length of fat quarter. Subcut:

- Each of 3 strips into 4 rectangles 1½″ × 4½″ (12 total).

- Each of 2 strips into 2 rectangles 1½″ × 8½″ (4 total).

- The remaining strip into 4 rectangles 1½″ × 3½″.

GREEN FABRIC 3

Cut 8 strips 1½″ × length of fat quarter. Subcut:

- Each of 4 strips into 2 rectangles 1½″ × 4½″ (8 total) and 1 rectangle 1½″ × 8½″ (4 total).

- Each of 4 strips into 1 rectangle 1½″ × 7½″ and 1 rectangle 1½″ × 10½″ (total of 4 each).

GREEN FABRIC 4

Cut 12 strips 1½″ × length of fat quarter. Subcut:

- Each of 4 strips into 1 rectangle 1½″ × 4½″ and 1 rectangle 1½″ × 11½″ (total of 4 each).

- Each of 4 strips into 1 rectangle 1½″ × 4½″ and 1 rectangle 1½″ × 12½″ (total of 4 each).

- Each of 4 strips into 1 rectangle 1½″ × 12½″ (4 total).

GREEN FABRIC 5

Cut 14 strips 1½″ × length of fat quarter. Subcut:

- Each of 2 strips into 4 rectangles 1½″ × 4½″ (8 total).

- Each of 4 strips into 1 rectangle 1½″ × 14½″ (4 total).

- Each of 4 strips into 1 rectangle 1½″ × 15½″ (4 total).

- Each of 4 strips into 1 rectangle 1½″ × 16½″ (4 total).

The remainder of the cutting instructions assume a 40″ WOF, but if your fabric is wider you may be able to fit these cuts into fewer strips. If being frugal with your fabric is important to you, read through the cutting instructions first and see what fits best with your WOF.

PINK FABRIC 1

Cut 7 strips 1½″ × WOF. Subcut:

- Each of 2 strips into 2 rectangles 1½″ × 16½″ (4 total) and 1 rectangle 1½″ × 4½″ (2 total).

- Each of 4 strips into 1 rectangle 1½″ × 20½″ and 1 rectangle 1½″ × 19½″ (total of 4 each).

- From the remaining strip, cut 6 rectangles 1½″ × 4½″.

PINK FABRIC 2

Cut 10 strips 1½″ × WOF. Subcut:

- Each of 2 strips into 2 rectangles 1½″ × 18½″ (4 total).

- Each of 4 strips into 1 rectangle 1½″ × 24½″ (4 total) and 2 rectangles 1½″ × 4½″ (8 total).

- Each of the remaining 4 strips into 4 rectangles 1½″ × 23½″.

PINK FABRIC 3

Cut 12 strips 1½″ × WOF. Subcut:

- Each of 2 strips into 1 rectangle 1½″ × 20½″ (2 total) and 4 rectangles 1½″ × 4½″ (8 total).

- Each of 2 strips into 1 rectangle 1½″ × 20½″ (2 total).

- Each of 4 strips into 1 rectangle 1½″ × 27½″ (4 total).

- Each of 4 strips into 1 rectangle 1½″ × 28½″ (4 total).

PINK FABRIC 4

Cut 12 strips 1½″ × WOF. Subcut:

- Each of 4 strips into 1 rectangle 1½″ × 22½″ (4 total) and 2 rectangles 1½″ × 4½″ (8 total).

- Each of 4 strips into 1 rectangle 1½″ × 31½″ (4 total).

- Each of 4 strips into 1 rectangle 1½″ × 32½″ (4 total).

PINK FABRIC 5

Cut 12 strips 1½″ × WOF. Subcut:

- Each of 4 strips into 1 rectangle 1½″ × 24½″ (4 total) and 2 rectangles 1½″ × 4½″ (8 total).

- Each of 4 strips into 1 rectangle 1½″ × 35½″ (4 total).

- Each of 4 strips into 1 rectangle 1½″ × 36½″ (4 total).

ORANGE FABRIC

Cut 8 strips 1½″ × length of fabric. Subcut:

- Each of 4 strips into 1 rectangles 1½″ × 40½″ (4 total).

- Each of 4 strips into 1 rectangles 1½″ × 39½″ (4 total).

CONSTRUCTION

Seam allowances are ¼".

After you piece the core and get comfortable with the technique for adding the series of borders, you'll find that this is a very easy quilt to make. The construction is similar to making Courthouse Steps, where strips are added to 2 opposite sides at the same time.

Assembling the Core

1. Sew green fabric 1 rectangles 1½" × 4½" to opposite sides of 2 gray 4½" × 4½" squares.

2. Sew the units from Step 1 to a gray 4½" × 6½" rectangle and press in the direction of the arrows.

3. Sew a green fabric 1 rectangle 1½" × 3½" to 1 side of each of 4 gray 3½" × 3½" squares.

4. Sew the units from Step 3 to 2 gray 3½" × 4½" rectangles.

5. Sew the units from Steps 2 and 4 together and press in the direction of the arrows.

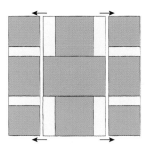

Piecing the Border Blocks

Each round of borders has 2 sections, A and B, which contain 2 units of equal size, for a total of 4.

Making Border 1

> **NOTE:** All odd-numbered borders are the narrower colored borders.

Group A: Sew a green fabric 2 outer "arm" 1½" × 3½" onto each short side of a green fabric 1 center 1½" × 6½". Press the seams toward the outer arms. Make 2.

Group B: Sew a green fabric 2 outer arm 1½" × 4½" onto each short side of a green fabric 1 center 1½" × 6½". Press the seams toward the outer arms. Make 2.

Making Border 2

> **NOTE:** All even-numbered borders are the wider gray borders.

Group A: Sew a 1½" × 4½" vertical "brace" onto each short side of a 4½" × 6½" gray center. Press toward the center. Sew a 3½" × 4½" gray arm onto each 4½" side of a green fabric 2 brace. Press toward the center. Make 2.

Group B: Sew a 1½" × 4½" green fabric 2 brace onto each short side of a 4½" × 6½" gray center. Press toward the center. Make 2.

From here on, use the chart to put the borders together.

BORDER #	CENTER FABRIC AND SIZE 2 EACH	ARM FABRIC AND SIZE 4 EACH	BRACE FABRIC AND SIZE 4 EACH
3A	Green 2, 1½″ × 8½″	Green 3, 1½″ × 7½″	
3B	Green 2, 1½″ × 8½″	Green 3, 1½″ × 8½″	
4A	Gray, 4½″ × 8½″	Gray, 4½″ × 7½″	Green 3, 1½″ × 4½″
4B	Gray, 4½″ × 8½″	Gray, 4½″ × 11½″	Green 3, 1½″ × 4½″
5A	Green 3, 1½″ × 10½″	Green 4, 1½″ × 11½″	
5B	Green 3, 1½″ × 10½″	Green 4, 1½″ × 12½″	
6A	Gray, 4½″ × 10½″	Gray, 4½″ × 11½″	Green 4, 1½″ × 4½″
6B	Gray, 4½″ × 10½″	Gray, 4½″ × 15½″	Green 4, 1½″ × 4½″
7A	Green 4, 1½″ × 12½″	Green 5, 1½″ × 15½″	
7B	Green 4, 1½″ × 12½″	Green 5, 1½″ × 16½″	
8A	Gray, 4½″ × 12½″	Gray, 4½″ × 15½″	Green 5, 1½″ × 4½″
8B	Gray, 4½″ × 12½″	Gray, 4½″ × 19½″	Green 5, 1½″ × 4½″
9A	Green 5, 1½″ × 14½″	Pink 1, 1½″ × 19½″	
9B	Green 5, 1½″ × 14½″	Pink 1, 1½″ × 20½″	
10A	Gray, 4½″ × 14½″	Gray, 4½″ × 19½″	Pink 1, 1½″ × 4½″
10B	Gray, 4½″ × 14½″	Gray, 4½″ × 23½″	Pink 1, 1½″ × 4½″
11A	Pink 1, 1½″ × 16½″	Pink 2, 1½″ × 23½″	
11B	Pink 1, 1½″ × 16½″	Pink 2, 1½″ × 24½″	

BORDER #	CENTER FABRIC AND SIZE 2 EACH	ARM FABRIC AND SIZE 4 EACH	BRACE FABRIC AND SIZE 4 EACH
12A	Gray, 4½" × 16½"	Gray, 4½" × 23½"	Pink 2, 1½" × 4½"
12B	Gray, 4½" × 16½"	Gray, 4½" × 27½"	Pink 2, 1½" × 4½"
13A	Pink 2, 1½" × 18½"	Pink 3, 1½" × 27½"	
13B	Pink 2, 1½" × 18½"	Pink 3, 1½" × 28½"	
14A	Gray, 4½" × 18½"	Gray, 4½" × 27½"	Pink 3, 1½" × 4½"
14B	Gray, 4½" × 18½"	Gray, 4½" × 31½"	Pink 3, 1½" × 4½"
15A	Pink 3, 1½" × 20½"	Pink 4, 1½" × 31½"	
15B	Pink 3, 1½" × 20½"	Pink 4, 1½" × 32½"	
16A	Gray, 4½" × 20½"	Gray, 4½" × 31½"	Pink 4, 1½" × 4½"
16B	Gray, 4½" × 20½"	Gray, 4½" × 35½"	Pink 4, 1½" × 4½"
17A	Pink 4, 1½" × 22½"	Pink 5, 1½" × 35½"	
17B	Pink 4, 1½" × 22½"	Pink 5, 1½" × 36½"	
18A	Gray, 4½" × 22½"	Gray, 4½" × 35½"	Pink 5, 1½" × 4½"
18B	Gray, 4½" × 22½"	Gray, 4½" × 39½"	Pink 5, 1½" × 4½"
19A	Pink 5, 1½" × 24½"	Orange, 1½" × 39½"	
19B	Pink 5, 1½" × 24½"	Orange, 1½" × 40½"	

Piecing the Quilt Top

Piecing the quilt top is simple if you keep the borders in order. I will walk you through adding Border 1A and 1B, followed by Border 2A and 2B. From there you will easily be able to complete the quilt top, adding the remaining borders in order.

Adding Border 1A and 1B

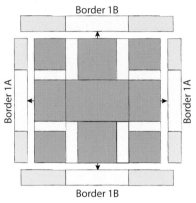

Add Border 1A and Border1B.

1. Sew Border 1A to the left and right sides of the core. Press the seams away from the core.

2. Sew Border 1B to the top and bottom.

> ### Tip
>
> I like to pin my seams where they nest and add pins to keep things nice and straight along the edges, as necessary.

3. Press the seams away from the core.

Adding Border 2A and 2B

Personally, I like to sew all the A borders on the same sides and all the B borders on the same sides, giving the quilt the look of Courthouse Steps and having the same seamlines throughout. If you forget, though, and add the next A border to the B border you just finished, it's no big deal!

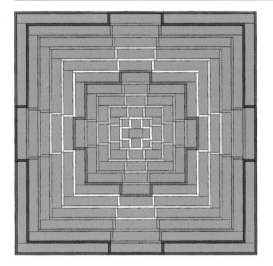

Orient the top so that the last border blocks, Border 1B, are at the top and bottom. Sew 1 Border 2A block to the left side of the top and 1 Border 2A block to the right. Press the seams outward.

Orient the top so that the Border 2A units are at the top and bottom. Nesting the seams and pinning as necessary, sew 1 Border 2B block to the left and 1 Border 2B block to the right. Press the seams outward.

Finishing

1. Layer the quilt top, batting, and backing and baste together the layers.

2. Quilt and bind.

Ancient cities are still standing and thriving, their histories leaving a lasting impression on their people.

Temple Steps

MADE BY Amanda Leins

FABRIC USED: Dottie and XOXO from RJR Fabrics, Cotton + Steel Basics from Cotton + Steel

Looking toward the Theater of Dionysus at the base of the Acropolis in Athens

Temple architecture in the ancient Mediterranean is visually powerful and they never cease to make me slow down and contemplate whenever I see them. Who were the people who had passed across the steps before me? What did this building witness in all its long years? Here I was, thousands of years later, traveling across the sometimes-broken stones that most likely had only been crossed by the feet of priests and priestesses in ancient times.

Many of the steps are broken, but their gracefulness is visible in what remains.

Materials

I chose to keep each color group together in the blocks, but this quilt would also look great if you alternated solid-color strips for a more rainbow effect. This quilt is well suited for using all solids or tone-on-tone prints, making the design stand out even more boldly.

- BACKGROUND (GRAY): 5¾ yards
- PINK: ⅜ yard
- PURPLE: ½ yard
- AQUA: ½ yard

- SALMON: ½ yard
- NAVY: ⅝ yard
- GREEN: ½ yard
- BATTING: 38″ × 114″

- BACKING: 3¼ yards
- BINDING: ½ yard
- SPRAY STARCH

Cutting

Note: It is crucial that you heavily starch the fabric before cutting to control the bias edges when piecing the top.

WOF=width of fabric

BACKGROUND

Cut 38 strips 2½″ × WOF; subcut 10 strips into half-strips 2½″ × 20″.

Cut 22 strips 1½″ × WOF; subcut 2 strips into half-strips 1½″ × 20″.

Cut 6 strips 9½″ × WOF.

AQUA AND PURPLE

Cut 10 strips 1½″ × WOF of each color.

PINK

Cut 8 strips 1½″ × WOF; subcut 3 into half-strips 1½″ × 20″.

SALMON AND GREEN

Cut 9 strips 1½″ × WOF; subcut 3 strips of each color into half-strips 1½″ × 20″.

NAVY

Cut 11 strips 1½″ × WOF; subcut 2 strips into half-strips 1½″ × 20″.

Who were the people who had
passed across the steps before me?

CONSTRUCTION

Seam allowances are ¼″.

Making the A Blocks

1. Beginning and ending with pink strips, sew together 5 pink strips 1½″ × WOF and 4 gray strips 1½″ × WOF, alternating between pink and gray. Offset each row by 2″. Press the seams in the direction of the arrows.

Block A

2. In a similar manner, make 2 aqua strip sets and 2 purple strip sets.

3. In a similar manner, use 5 pink 1½″ × 20″ half-strips and 4 gray 1½″ × 20″ half-strips to create a half-sized strip set.

4. Place a strip set horizontally and cut a 45° angle from the bottom right corner toward the top left.

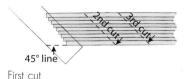

45° line

First cut

5. From this cut, mark 10⅝″ intervals along the bottom length of the strip set. Cut the same 45° angle from lower right to upper left as before at each mark.

6. Cut 4 pink A blocks, 5 aqua A blocks, and 5 purple A blocks.

Making the B Blocks

Place a background-color 9½″ × WOF strip horizontally and cut a 45° angle from the bottom left corner to the upper right. Mark 10⅝″ intervals along the bottom length of the strip. Cut a 45° angle from the bottom left to the right at each mark to make a parallelogram. Each 40″ strip will provide 2 full B blocks and 1 partial block. Cut a total of 12 parallelograms.

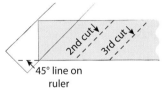

45° line on ruler

Block B

Making the C Blocks

1. Beginning and ending with gray strips, sew together 4 gray strips 2½″ × WOF and 3 salmon strips 1½″ × WOF, alternating between gray and salmon fabric. Offset each row by 2″. Press the seams in the direction of the arrows. Block C has the same 45° angle as block A.

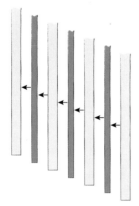

2. In a similar manner, make 2 navy strip sets and 1 green strip set.

3. Use 3 salmon 1½″ × 20″ half-strips and 4 gray 2½″ × 20″ half-strips to create a half-sized strip set.

4. In a similar manner, make 1 green half-sized strip set.

5. Place the strip horizontally as you did for the A blocks (page 66). Cut a 45° angle from the lower left corner toward the top right.

6. From this point, mark 10⅝″ intervals along the entire bottom length of the fabric and cut a 45° angle as before at each mark.

7. Cut 4 salmon C blocks, 5 navy C blocks, and 4 green C blocks.

Making the D Blocks

1. Beginning and ending with gray strips, sew together 4 gray strips 2½″ × WOF and 3 salmon strips 1½″ × WOF, alternating between gray and salmon. When adding the next strip, offset each row by 2″, as shown. Press the seams in the direction of the arrows. **Note:** Make sure you offset these strips correctly! They're different from blocks A and C.

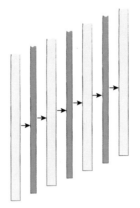

2. In the same manner, make 1 navy strip set and 1 green strip set.

3. Use the 20″-long strips to create 1 half-sized strip set each of salmon, navy, and green.

4. Place the strip sets horizontally and cut a 45° angle from the bottom left corner toward the top right.

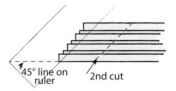

45° line on ruler   2nd cut

5. From this cut, mark 10⅝″ intervals along the bottom length of the strip set. Cut the same 45° angle as before at each mark.

6. Cut 4 blocks each of salmon, navy, and green.

ASSEMBLING THE TOP

1. Arrange the rows as shown in the quilt assembly diagram. Check to make sure that the seams will nest properly. If they won't, simply spin the block around and they will line up.

2. For each row, join the blocks together, short seams to short seams.

3. For odd-numbered rows, press the seams to the right. For even-numbered rows, press the seams to the left.

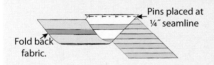

Pin Placement

Save yourself the hassle of ripping out imperfectly joined blocks with this trick: Use a couple of long pins to "audition" where the seam will be. As you gently turn the fabric back, you can see whether the fabric placement is correct.

Pins placed at ¼" seamline

Fold back fabric.

4. Sew together the rows. Note that the rows will not always line up perfectly at the top and bottom, and there will be points sticking out everywhere. This is okay: you'll be trimming off those points.

Tip

I like to sew 2 rows together at a time, using as many pins as necessary to keep things aligned. Then sew pairs together, and so on, until the entire top is done.

5. Sew a salmon block D to the top left and a green block D to the bottom right. Press the seams toward block D.

FINISHING

1. Place the top with Row 1 to the left and Row 13 to the right. The red line on the quilt assembly diagram (below) shows the location of the trim lines. If you wish to make your quilt top a little taller, there is room for that.

2. Square the top *right* corner and trim the length of the right side edge to 32˝; square the bottom left corner as well.

> ## Tip
>
> When squaring large tops like this that do not have straight lines to follow, I find one of those self-leveling laser levels to be absolutely the best tool in the world! I use my gridded mat to set up the main guideline to be a perfect 90° before cutting.

3. With the 2 opposite corners perfectly square, work your way across the top of the quilt, trimming the width of the quilt.

4. Layer the quilt top, batting, and backing and baste together the layers.

5. Quilt and bind.

Quilt assembly

Tessellation

PATTERN DESIGNED BY Amanda Leins; made by Susan Bishop

FABRIC USED: Peppered Cottons from Studio E Fabrics

Early Roman mosaics often featured tessellations, geometric patterns that repeat indefinitely with no overlaps and no gaps. Even the simplest, like this one, draws you in as your eye follows the shapes around, trying to pick out connections and patterns in color and line.

One of the lovely things about tessellations is the opportunity to play with a variety of colors.

Two aspects of color are particularly important:

Hue: The name of the color as it appears (purple, blue-green, orange).

Value: How light or dark a hue is. Value is critical in seeing patterns because it is the contrast in values that makes patterns apparent.

For this quilt, I provided my friend Susan Bishop with fabric that had light and dark values. Notice that the top of the quilt looks very orderly because each row uses two hues, one light and one dark. In the middle of the quilt, it is mostly regular with a few variations thrown in. At the bottom of the quilt, the colors are more randomly placed and darker, providing contrast with the top of the quilt.

Another option for color selection would be to have rows of dark solid colors alternating with cream or other neutrals, creating a stripy effect.

Tip

If you ever have trouble selecting colors, I highly recommend Joen Wolfrom's *Ultimate 3-in-1 Color Tool* (Resources, page 110). I use it often to determine whether I like the look of certain color combinations. It also has a great primer at the beginning on color.

Materials

- **Squares and diamonds:** ⅔ yard each of 8 colors

- **Backing:** 3½ yards

- **Batting:** 63″ × 71″

- **Binding:** ⅔ yard

Cutting

For greatest accuracy, starch the fabrics before beginning. When cutting the diamonds, stack only 2 strips at most, to ensure a perfect angled cut.

WOF=width of fabric

SQUARES

- From each of 8 fabrics, cut 3 strips 3½″ × WOF; subcut 11 squares 3½″ × 3½″ from each strip, for a total of 264 squares.

DIAMONDS

- From each of 8 fabrics, cut 4 strips 2⅝″ × WOF; subcut 8–10 45° diamonds 2⅝″ × 3⅝″ from each strip. You need a total of 263 diamonds. It's nice to have some extras so you can tweak your design.

⟵ 3⅝″ ⟶

CONSTRUCTION

This quilt is constructed from 2 types of rows that alternate and are sewn together using Y-seams (see Sewing Y-Seams, page 76).

- The rows can begin with either diamonds or squares.

- For Row A, the square is always "flat," and the diamond always points up and to the left.

- For Row B, the square is always on point, and the diamond is always horizontal, with the point to the upper right, as shown.

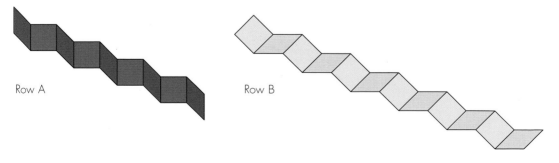

Row A

Row B

Making the Rows

Seam allowances are ¼˝.

1. Refer to the Sewing Chart for A and B Rows (below) for the number of diamonds and squares in each row and which shape to begin with.

2. To sew a row, begin ¼˝ from the top edge and stop ¼˝ from the bottom edge, backstitching or knotting off at both the beginning and the end. Take care that the shapes are in the correct position for the row you are working on. Do not press any seams yet!

If your presser foot does not have ¼˝ marks on it, refer to Using a Sticky Note to Mark ¼˝ Stop and Start (page 79).

Sewing Chart for A and B Rows

ROW	TOTAL NUMBER OF SQUARES	TOTAL NUMBER OF DIAMONDS	FIRST SHAPE IN ROW	LAST SHAPE IN ROW	NUMBER OF ROWS TO MAKE
A1	12	11	square	square	5
A2	11	12	diamond	diamond	2
A3	10	11	diamond	diamond	2
A4	8	8	square	diamond	2
A5	4	5	diamond	diamond	2
A6	2	2	square	diamond	2
B1	12	12	square	diamond	3
B2	11	12	diamond	diamond	2
B3	12	12	diamond	square	3
B4	10	9	square	square	2
B5	6	6	diamond	diamond	2
B6	4	3	square	square	2

Making the Quilt Top

Sew together the rows following the Row A and Row B top plans (below). Don't press until all the rows are sewn together.

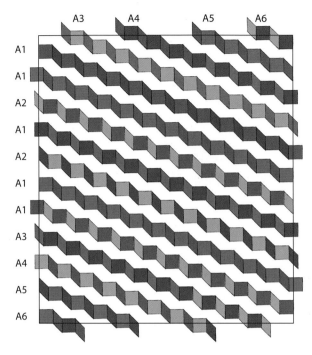

Row A top plan

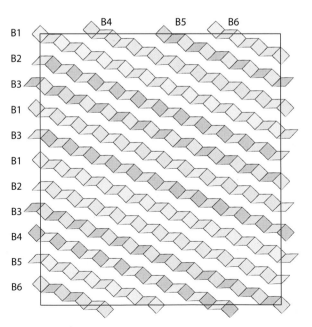

Row B top plan

Staystitching

The top has a fair amount of stretch along its sides, thanks to all those bias edges. In order to cut down on stretch and wavy edges, I highly recommend using a *stay stitch* to keep the fabric in place. It is very effective for controlling the edges. I use this on improv quilts for the same reason. Sew all the way around the quilt ⅛" from the cut edge. This way, the stay stitch will do its job and still be inside the ¼" seam allowance when you go to bind your quilt.

Early Roman mosaics often featured tessellations, geometric patterns that repeat indefinitely with no overlaps and no gaps.

Sewing Y-Seams

The trick to sewing Y-seams in this quilt is stopping at the already sewn seams (and not sewing over them) and backstitching or stitching in place to knot the ends of the thread so the seams don't come undone. I recommend using a fine thread (such as Bottom Line or Monopoly by Superior Threads) and backstitching at the beginning and end of each seam. If you do use Bottom Line or Monopoly, use a slightly lower temperature setting on your iron than for cotton when you press. Alternatively, at the beginning and end of each seam, shorten your stitch length to 1.4 or 1.5.

1. Beginning with the top left corner of the quilt top (Rows A6 and B6), orient the rows as shown.

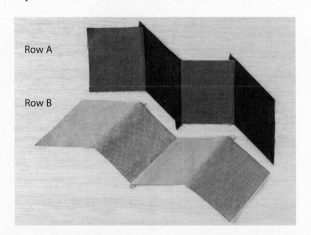

Row A

Row B

2. Flip Row A down over Row B, so both are right sides together. Align (match up) the unsewn edge of the first A square with the first B diamond, and nest the first seam intersection. Pin. Start sewing at the edge of the fabric and stop a few threads before the seam and backstitch or knot off.

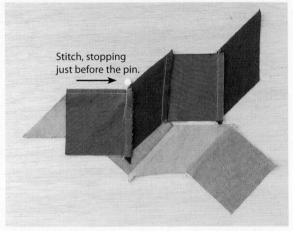

Stitch, stopping just before the pin.

3. Open up the rows and carefully fold the first A square in half diagonally, so that the next A diamond aligns with the B square. Move the seam allowances out of the way. Nest the next seam intersection, and pin.

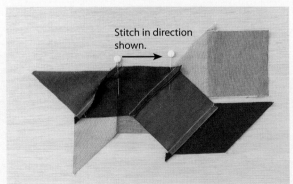

Stitch in direction shown.

4. Begin sewing a thread or 2 away from the previous seamline, backstitch or knot off, and sew to a thread or 2 from the next seamline (this should also be approximately ¼″ in from the corners). Backstitch or knot off.

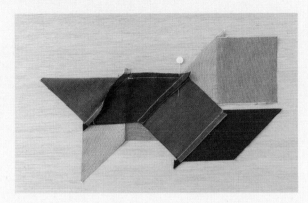

5. Repeat with each seam until you reach the end of a row.

6. For the final seam, sew to the end.

Finishing

1. Press from the back side of the quilt top, working from the top right corner. Move across the quilt top, pressing the seams as they naturally fall.

2. Layer the quilt top, batting, and backing and baste together the layers.

3. Quilt as desired.

4. Trim the edges as shown and bind.

Quilt assembly and trimming

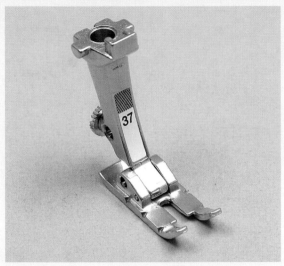

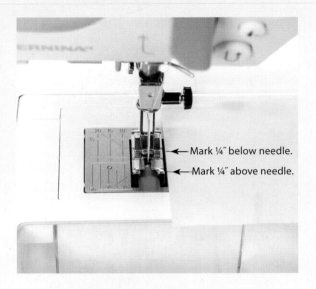

Mark ¼″ below needle.

Mark ¼″ above needle.

Bernina foot with ¼″ markings

You may want to mark the corners of the cut pieces to show where you need to begin and end ¼″ from an edge. My ¼″ foot, however, has markings that indicate where ¼″ is both before and behind the needle position. If your ¼″ foot does not have these markings, you can make your own guide with a sticky note.

I like to line up the edge of the sticky note along the edge of where my ¼″ seam would be and fasten it down on the right with a piece of blue tape to prevent shifting. I then use the lines on the bed of my machine and throat plate to align a ruler or piece of cardstock with the needle and mark the exact point where the needle falls. Using my gridded ruler, I mark horizontal lines ¼″ *above and below* the needle marking.

The top mark is where I line up the top edge of the block so that when I lower the needle it is ¼″ from the corner. The bottom mark is where I stop sewing when the bottom edge of the block lines up.

Test your lines by marking a block ¼″ from the top and bottom right-side corners. Drop your needle at the top mark and sew to the bottom, stopping when the bottom edge of the block lines up with the ¼″ mark on your sticky note, below the needle mark. Personally, when I can, I prefer to piece with the square on top, so that I can see where the corner is every time.

Mosaic Pillows

MADE BY Amanda Leins | **FABRIC USED:** Cherrywood Hand Dyed Fabrics, Kona Cotton Solids from Robert Kaufman Fabrics

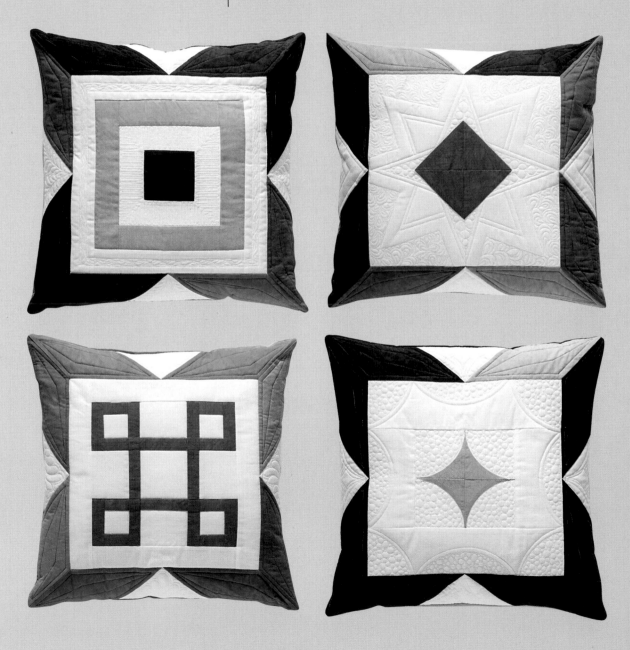

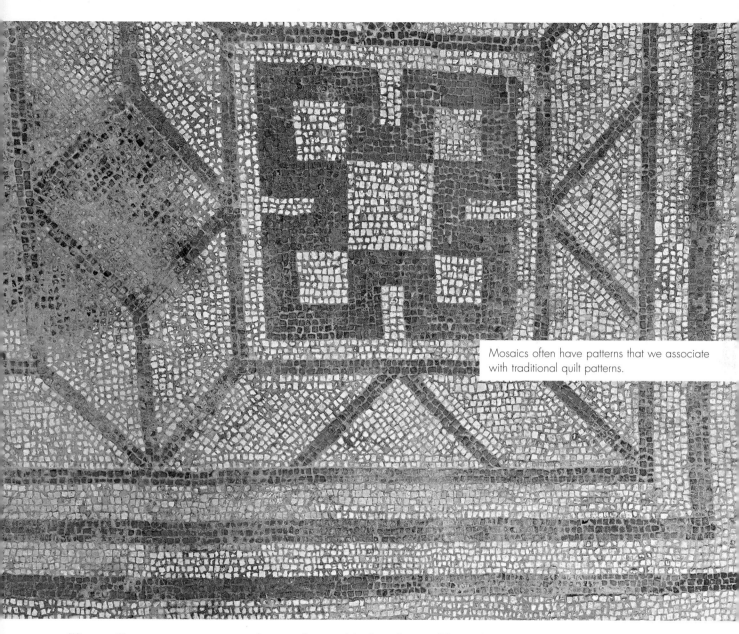

Mosaics often have patterns that we associate with traditional quilt patterns.

These pillows are a great way to frame a favorite block or design. The technique used to create the frames shows you how to sew mitered corners, which are also used in *Lovely Fishbourne* (page 90). The pillows are made using four blocks from *Lovely Fishbourne*, one for each pillow, but feel free to branch out and use other patterns.

If you don't want pillows, you can join together the blocks to make a table runner or small wallhanging.

Photo © Fishbourne Roman Palace/Sussex Archaeological Society

Materials

Makes 4 pillows

- **BORDER FABRICS (PARALLELOGRAMS FOR PILLOW CORNERS, AS SHOWN):**
  ¾ yard total for borders, either yardage or fat quarters *(When cutting, you will get 2 parallelograms from each strip cut along the length of a fat quarter and 5 parallelograms from each strip cut along the width of the yardage.)*
- **BRIGHT-COLOR FABRICS FOR INTERIOR BLOCK DESIGNS (AS SHOWN):** Assorted scraps (Refer to Cutting, below, for specifics.)
- **WHITE:** 1⅛ yard
- **MUSLIN:** 2¼ yards
- **BATTING:** 53″ × 53″ or 4 pieces at least 24″ × 24″
- **PILLOW BACKING:** 1½ yards
- **PILLOW FORMS:** 4 at 18″ × 18″

Cutting

NOTE: Starching your fabrics will make it easier to construct these blocks accurately.

WOF=width of fabric

Each pillow requires 8 angled arms/parallelograms and 4 quarter-square triangles, for a total of 32 arms and 16 quarter-square triangles. If you're going scrappy, this should help you determine your cutting needs.

BORDERS

Parallelograms for corners

Cut strips 3½″ × WOF from yardage or 3½″ × length of fat quarters (the number of strips needed will depend on whether you are using yardage or fat quarters and the number of colors); subcut 32 parallelograms (8 for each pillow) as follows:

Place the strips horizontally on a cutting mat, stacking no more than 2 at a time. Cut at 45°.

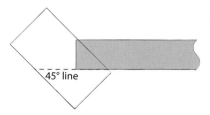

From the cut point, mark 6¾″ as many times as you can along the top and bottom edges, and cut on a 45° angle at each point. Cut a total of 32 parallelograms.

White quarter-square triangles

Cut 2 strips 7½″ × WOF; subcut 4 squares 7½″ × 7½″ and then cut each square in half on the diagonal twice to make a total of 16 quarter-square triangles.

INTERIOR BLOCKS

Pillow 1 (Snowball variation)

Bright color: Cut 4 squares 3½″ × 3½″.

White: Cut 1 strip 6½″ × WOF; subcut 4 squares 6½″ × 6½″.

Pillow 2 (Square-in-a-Square)

Bright color: Cut 1 square 3½″ × 3½″ and 1 rectangle 2″ × WOF; subcut 2 rectangles 2″ × 6½″ and 2 rectangles 2″ × 9½″.

White: Cut 2 strips 2″ × WOF. From each strip, subcut 1 rectangle 2″ × 3½″, 1 rectangle 2″ × 6½″, 1 rectangle 2″ × 9½″, and 1 rectangle 2″ × 12½″ (total of 2 each).

Pillow 3 (Roman Knot)

Bright color: Cut 2 strips 1¼″ × WOF. From each strip, subcut 4 rectangles 1¼″ × 2″ (8 total) and 6 rectangles 1¼″ × 3½″ (12 total).

White: Cut 2 strips 2″ × WOF; subcut 4 squares 2″ × 2″, 2 rectangles 2″ × 9½″, and 2 rectangles 2″ × 12½″.

Cut 1 strip 3½″ × WOF; subcut 1 square 3½″ × 3½″ and 4 rectangles 2¾″ × 3½″.

Pillow 4 (Drunkard's Path variation)

Bright color: Cut 1 strip 3½″ × WOF; subcut 4 arch pieces using Drunkard's Path Pattern A (page P2).

White: Cut 2 strips 3½″ × WOF. From the first strip, subcut 4 quarter-circles using Drunkard's Path Pattern B (page P2) and 2 rectangles 3½″ × 6½″. From the remaining strip, subcut 2 rectangles 3½″ × 12½″.

PILLOW BACKS

Cut 4 pieces 13″ × WOF; subcut each piece into 2 rectangles 13″ × 18½″, for a total of 8 rectangles.

Muslin: Cut 4 squares 20″ × 20″.

CONSTRUCTION

Seam allowances are ¼".

Tip

If you're making pillows with scrappy borders, lay them out first to make sure you're happy with the fabric placement.

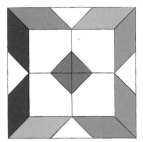

Snowball variation

Square-in-a-Square

Roman Knot

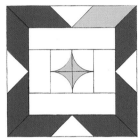

Drunkard's Path variation

Making Pillow 1

Snowball Variation

This is a variation on the traditional Snowball block.

1. Mark a diagonal line from corner to corner on the wrong side of 4 bright-color 3½" × 3½" squares.

2. Place the marked square right sides together in the corner of a white 6½" × 6½" square and pin.

3. Sew on the marked diagonal line. Trim ¼" from the seamline. Press toward the white.

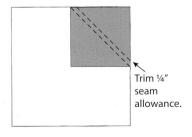

Trim ¼" seam allowance.

Tip

When pressing seams toward the white fabric, if the bright colors shadow through, I recommend grading the seams (trimming the color seam allowance) to reduce the shadowing.

4. Repeat to make a total of 4 blocks.

5. Sew together pairs of the Snowball blocks so that the corners with color join in the middle. Press the seams in opposite directions on each block. Sew together the 2 halves. Press the seam allowance to one side.

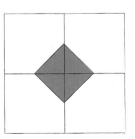

These pillows are a great way to frame a favorite block or design.

Making Pillow 2

Square-in-a-Square

1. Sew 2 white 2″ × 3½″ rectangles to opposite sides of a bright-color 3½″ × 3½″ square.

2. Sew 2 white 2″ × 6½″ rectangles to opposite sides of the unit from Step 1.

3. Continue building outward with the remaining strips, pressing the seams toward the outer edges of the block and referring to the photo (page 84) as needed.

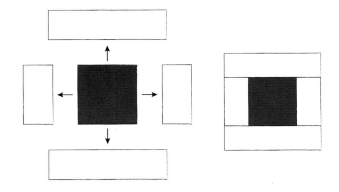

Making Pillow 3

Roman Knot

1. Sew 2 bright-color 1¼″ × 2″ rectangles to opposite sides of a white 2″ × 2″ square. Press the seam allowances toward the rectangles.

2. Sew 2 bright-color 1¼″ × 3½″ rectangles to the remaining sides of the square. Press the seam allowances toward the rectangles.

3. Repeat to make a total of 4 blocks.

4. Sew a bright-color 1¼″ × 3½″ rectangle to a white 2¾″ × 3½″ rectangle. Press the seam toward the colored rectangle. Repeat to make a total of 4 blocks.

5. Arrange all the units with the 3½″ × 3½″ white squares in the center, as shown in the pillow block assembly diagram (at right).

6. Sew together the rows. For Rows 1 and 3, press the seam allowances toward the middle. For Row 2, press the seams toward the outside.

7. Sew together the rows, spinning the seams where they meet (refer to Spinning Seams, page 100).

8. Complete the block by sewing 2 white 2″ × 9½″ strips to opposite sides of the block. Press the seam allowances outward.

9. Sew 2 white 2″ × 12½″ rectangles to the remaining sides to complete the square. Press the seam allowances outward.

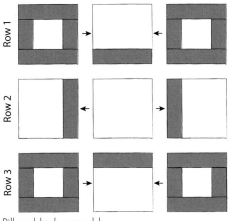

Pillow block assembly

Making Pillow 4

Drunkard's Path Variation

1. Sew 1 quarter-circle of the Drunkard's Path block to the corresponding arch (Refer to Piecing Half-Circles, page 18). Repeat to make 4.

2. Align the blocks so the arches mirror each other and sew them together. Press the seam allowances to the right.

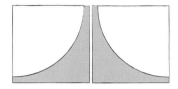

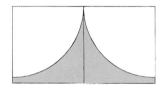

3. Repeat with the remaining 2 blocks.

4. Finish the block by nesting the seams and sewing the 2 halves together down the center. Press to the side and spin the seams (see Spinning Seams, page 100).

5. Sew 2 white 3½″ × 6½″ rectangles to opposite sides of the Drunkard's Path block. Press the seam allowances outward.

6. Sew 2 white 3½″ × 12½″ rectangles to the other 2 sides. Press the seam allowances outward.

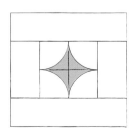

Making the Borders

1. Sew together a border parallelogram and a white quarter-square triangle.

2. Press the seam allowances toward the parallelogram.

3. Sew a second parallelogram to the other side of the quarter-square triangle.

4. Press toward the parallelogram and trim the points.

5. Repeat to make a total of 16 borders.

Sewing Borders with Mitered Corners to Blocks

1. Line up the point of the quarter-square triangle in the border with the middle of the interior block and pin, right sides together.

2. Mark ¼″ in from each edge. Sew a seam beginning and ending at the ¼″ mark. Backstitch at each point or shorten the stitch length to 1.4 or 1.5 at the beginning and end of the seam.

3. Press toward the outer border.

4. Repeat with the remaining 3 sides.

5. Starting with a corner, fold the pillow top right sides together so the mitered edges line up exactly; gently move the fabric of the pillow top and the seam allowances out of the way.

6. Beginning at the outer corner, sew using a short stitch length to a point just inside the previous seamlines, usually a thread's width or 2 away. Repeat for the remaining corners. Backstitch or use a shorter stitch length.

Note: Be precise! Sewing even a thread over the previous seams, or even the seam allowances, will result in a noticeable pucker. Not sewing close enough to the seam allowance will result in a gap in the corner.

Preparing the Pillow Backs

1. Fold over the short edge of 1 backing 13″ × 18½″ rectangle to the wrong side by ½″. Press firmly.

2. Fold over the edge a second time by ½″ and press firmly.

3. Topstitch along the edge to secure in place.

4. Repeat for the remaining rectangles. Make 8.

Finishing the Pillows

1. Quilt the pillow tops using muslin as the backing.

2. Trim the quilted pillow tops to 18½″ × 18½″ square.

3. Using a gridded mat, place the pillow backs to fit within an 18½″ square with right sides facing up, overlapping the finished edges in the middle.

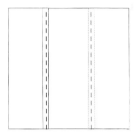

4. Carefully place a quilted pillow top over the pillow backing, right sides together. All 4 sides should match up. Pin the pieces in place.

5. Sew a ¼″ seam around the entire perimeter of the pillow, reinforcing at the corners and the envelope opening with backstitching if you wish.

6. Trim the corners if desired. Turn right side out and insert the pillow form.

7. Repeat Steps 3–6 for the other 3 pillows.

Lovely Fishbourne

PIECED BY Amanda Leins; quilted by Liz Haskell | **FABRIC USED:** Cherrywood Hand Dyed Fabrics

Mosaic from Fishbourne Roman Palace, 1st century AD

With its collection of amazing mosaics and multitude of rooms, Fishbourne Palace, located in Sussex, England, is a truly remarkable archaeological site. Managed by the Sussex Archaeological Society, it is the grandest Roman palace in Britain, with a history spanning centuries. Despite its existence far from the center of the Roman Empire, it is filled with all the comforts and details of the grand villas on the Italian peninsula, and to visit it is to see a perfect example of how the Romans carried their cultural identity with them no matter where they settled. For its inhabitants, it acted as an outward sign of their greatness, while also acting as a remembrance of a home far away.

One mosaic in particular, to me as a quilter, is a metaphor for the quilting world. Looking at it the first time, I got a chill when I recognized designs such as the LeMoyne Star, Square-in-a-Square, and other blocks so closely tied with American quilts. Considered to be hallmarks of traditional blocks, these designs have been part of our language of pattern for eons. I felt a strong sense of connection between all of us who see beauty and pattern everywhere, and I hope you will turn these traditional patterns into your own work of art in cloth and thread.

Photo © Fishbourne Roman Palace/Sussex Archaeological Society

Materials

- **WHITE:** 5¼ yards
- **BLOCKS:** 2 yards total (I used 8 fat quarters in harmonious analogous colors—the Blue Lagoon bundle from Cherrywood—for the block pieces.)

- **INNER BORDER (GREEN):** ⅝ yard
- **OUTER BORDER (BLUE):** ⅝ yard
- **BINDING:** ¾ yard
- **BACKING:** 8 yards
- **BATTING:** 95″ × 95″

Cutting

Use the patterns (pullout page P2) to make templates.

WOF=width of fabric

Tip

This top is about precision and patience and enjoying the process. Take the time to do it right—use starch when preparing your fabrics to help control the bias edges so you can get precise cuts. If you glue baste, this is the time to use that technique, because it will provide absolute control over those bias edges as you sew. Make your decisions about colors and values and where you want to use them so that you can cut what you need and then arrange the pieces according to your desires before you begin to sew.

I wanted the elements that were not star arms to stand out the most: light colors pop out and darker colors recede.

WHITE

Label the pieces by size as you cut them so you can easily find them.

Cut 16 strips 2″ × WOF.

- From 1 strip, subcut 6 rectangles 2″ × 6½″.
- From 1 strip, subcut 8 rectangles 2″ × 3½″. Use the rest of the strip to begin cutting the Flying Geese triangles using Flying Geese Triangle B (pattern pullout page P2).
- From 1 strip, cut the remaining Flying Geese triangles (16 Triangle A, 16 Triangle B).
- From 1 strip, subcut 4 rectangles 2″ × 9½″.
- From 2 strips, subcut 8 rectangles 2″ × 9¾″.
- Set aside the remaining 10 strips for the borders.

Cut 3 strips 3½″ × WOF.

- From 1 strip, subcut 1 chisel with a 45° angle at an end measuring 3½″ × 12⅞″ along the longest length and 1 chisel with a 45° angle at an end measuring 3½″ × 9⅞″ along the longest length.

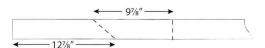

- From 1 strip, subcut 1 rectangle 3½″ × 12½″ and 4 Drunkard's Path Pattern A pieces.

Cut 1 strip 4½″ × WOF; subcut 1 rectangle 4½″ × 39½″.

Cut 1 strip 7¼″ × WOF; subcut 4 squares 7¼″ × 7¼″ and then cut them on the diagonal twice to make 8 quarter-square triangles.

Cut 2 strips 6½″ × WOF.

- From 1 strip, subcut 2 squares 6½″ × 6½″ and 1 rectangle 6½″ × 18½″; from the remainder, subcut 1 square 3⅞″ × 3⅞″ and then cut it on the diagonal to make 2 half-square triangles.

- From the second strip, subcut 1 rectangle 6½″ × 30½″ and 1 rectangle 6½″ × 9½″.

Cut 1 strip 9½″ × WOF; subcut 1 rectangle 9½″ × 15½″ and 1 rectangle 6½″ × 15½″.

Cut 1 strip 6⅞″ × WOF; subcut 2 squares 6⅞″ × 6⅞″ and then cut them on the diagonal to make 4 half-square triangles.

Cut 1 strip 58½″ × WOF; subcut 1 rectangle 23″ × 58½″ and 1 rectangle 17″ × 58½″.

Cut 2 strips 20½″ × WOF; subcut each into 1 rectangle 20½″ × 39½″ (2 total) and then sew together the 2 rectangles along the 20½″ edges to make a single piece 20½″ × 78½″.

BLOCKS

Star arms

Cut strips 3½″ × WOF from yardage or 3½″ × length of fat quarters (the number of strips needed will depend on whether you are using yardage or fat quarters and the number of colors). Each fat-quarter strip has enough fabric for 2 star arms, and each yardage strip has enough fabric for 5 star arms.

Subcut 28 star arms as follows:

1. Place the strips horizontally.

2. Mark a point on the top left edge for the first cut. From that point, measure 6¾″ and mark a point. This will be the location of the next angled cut. Continue until you have marked all the possible star arms.

3. Beginning at the left, align your grid ruler with the 45° mark along the bottom left. Slide the ruler until the entire area you wish to cut is covered and the top edge of the ruler meets your first mark. Cut a 45° angle at each point.

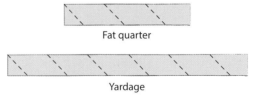

Fat quarter

Yardage

Cutting star arms from a fat quarter or yardage

Flying Geese Cross

Cut 1 strip 3½″ × WOF; subcut 16 geese using Flying Geese Pattern C and 4 quarter-circles using Drunkard's Path Pattern B.

Diamond-in-a-Square

Cut 1 square 4¾″ × 4¾″ for the diamond.

Cut 2 squares 5⅛″ × 5⅛″ and then cut it on the diagonal to make 4 half-square triangles.

Square-in-a-Square

Cut 1 square 3½″ × 3½″.

Cut 4 rectangles 3½″ × 9½″.

Simple Cross

From each color, cut 2 rectangles 3½″ × 8″.

Rectangle-in-a-Rectangle

Cut 2 rectangles 3½″ × 9½″.

BORDERS

For each border, cut 10 strips 2″ × WOF. Sew short ends to short ends. Press the seam allowances toward one side. This way, you can easily cut the lengths you need and all the seams will land in different locations.

CONSTRUCTION

Seam allowances are ¼″.

Tips

- I highly recommend using a design wall—it helps to see where everything goes as you're sewing.

- To minimize the bulk from backstitching, use a smaller stitch length, from 1.6 to 1.8. You can use an even smaller stitch if you want, but it's best not to go smaller than your seam ripper can handle!

- Take photos of your layout to remind yourself where the pieces belong.

Making the Flying Geese Cross Block

1. Sew 1 white triangle A to a colored triangle as shown. Press toward the white triangle.

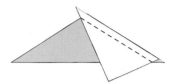

2. Sew a white triangle B on the opposite side. Press toward the white triangle.

3. Make 16 Flying Geese blocks.

4. Sew the geese together in groups of 4, pressing the seams away from the tips.

5. Sew 4 Drunkard's Path blocks (refer to Piecing Half-Circles, page 18).

6. Sew together 2 blocks so that a point forms at the seam.

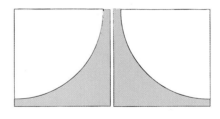

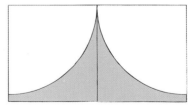

7. Repeat with the remaining 2 blocks and press the seams open.

8. Sew together the 2 halves. Press the seams open.

Making the Rectangle-in-a-Rectangle Blocks

1. Sew white 2″ × 9½″ rectangles to opposite sides of 1 colored 3½″ × 9½″ rectangle. Press the seam allowances toward the colored fabric.

2. Sew white 2″ × 6½″ rectangles to opposite sides of the block from Step 1. Press the seam allowances toward the outside of the block.

3. Repeat to make 2.

Making the Star Blocks

All the star blocks start with the same star core. After that, each star has different inset squares and rectangles. There are 4 star variations.

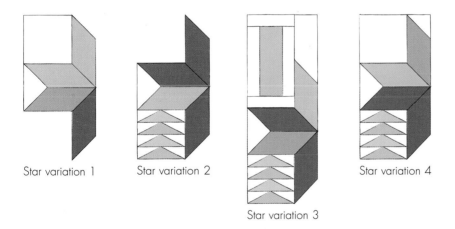

Star variation 1   Star variation 2   Star variation 4

Star variation 3

For all 4 star variations:

1. Sew together 1 white 7¼″ quarter-square triangle and 1 star arm. Press toward the arm.

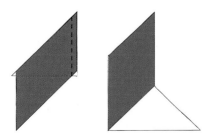

2. With the white quarter-square triangle facing up, sew the next arm as shown, starting ¼″ from the outer edge and sewing toward the point of the quarter-square triangle; carefully move the seam allowance away from the seamline. **Note:** Use the previous line of stitching as a guide for where to stop sewing; it should also be just shy of ¼″ from the tip of the quarter-square triangle. Stop a thread or 2 before, as stitching too near the seam or over the seam allowance will result in a pucker; stopping too far away will result in a hole.

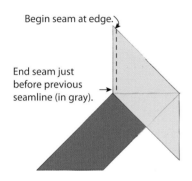

3. Press the seam allowance toward the quarter-square triangle.

4. Line up the interior edges of the arms from the point of the quarter-square triangle to the tips of the arms. Gently work the quarter-square triangle so that the right-side face is pulled back and out of the way, and gently pull back the seam allowances. Pin the arms in place and sew from the tips of the arms to just before the previous lines of stitching at the tip of the quarter-square triangle. Open and check for puckers or gaps; then press the seam allowance toward the right-side arm. This forms the core of the star blocks.

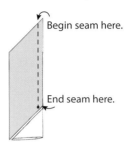

Note how the quarter-square triangle is folded in half.

Completed star core

5. With the quarter-square triangle to the left and the arms pointing to the right, facing right side up, sew a new arm beginning ¼″ from the outer edge to the point as shown. Press the seam allowance toward the new arm. Repeat on the other side. Make 4 star cores.

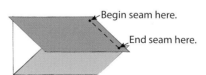

Star Variation 1

This star is the left border for the Diamond-in-a-Square.

1. Arrange the star core right side up with the outer arms spread at the bottom to the right and left.

2. To prepare the inset square, align 1 white 6½˝ × 6½˝ square with the *right edge* of the vertical core. Pin in place.

3. Sew from the upper right edge, stopping just before the seamline at the corner. Press the seam allowance toward the vertical core.

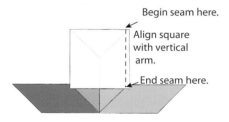

Begin seam here.
Align square with vertical arm.
End seam here.

4. Finish sewing the inset square by aligning the remaining edges of the square and the lower right arm; move the star arms around as necessary. Pin as needed to keep things in place.

5. Begin sewing from the outer edge of the square; stop ¼˝ from the interior corner.

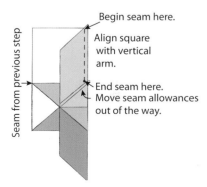

Begin seam here.
Align square with vertical arm.
Seam from previous step
End seam here.
Move seam allowances out of the way.

Star Variation 2

This star is the bottom of the Diamond-in-a-Square and the far right of the Flying Geese Cross.

1. Arrange the star core as in Step 1 of Star Variation 1 (at left).

2. Arrange the Flying Geese block so that the geese point to the *left side* of the star core. The first seam will be where the core and the Flying Geese block align.

3. Beginning at the outer edge, sew toward the interior corner; stop just before the seamline. Press the seam allowances toward the core.

4. Line up the bottom edge of the Flying Geese block and the edge of the star arm. Begin sewing from the outside edge; stop ¼˝ from the interior corner. Press the seam allowance toward the arm.

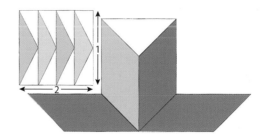

Star Variation 3

This star is inset between the Flying Geese Cross and the Rectangle-in-a-Rectangle.

1. Arrange the star core as in Step 1 of Star Variation 1 (page 97).

2. Sew the white 3½″ × 9⅞″ chisel to the right-side arm.

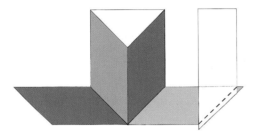

3. Inset the Flying Geese block as you did in Step 2 of Star Variation 2 (page 97).

4. To finish the block, align the short edge of the rectangle-in-a-rectangle with the right side of the star core.

5. Begin sewing from the top of the core; stop ¼″ from the interior corner.

6. Finish the block by aligning the long edge of the rectangle with the long edge of the star arm and chisel. Sew from the outside edge; stop ¼″ from the interior corner.

Star Variation 4

This star is inset with the Flying Geese block and the Square-in-a-Square.

1. Follow Steps 1–3 of Star Variation 2 (page 97).

2. Sew 1 white 3⅞″ half-square triangle to the right arm of the star block. Press the seam allowances toward the white.

3. Inset 1 white 6½″ × 6½″ square as shown.

Making the Simple Cross Block

1. Sew 1 white 2″ × 3½″ rectangle to a short end of a colored 3½″ × 8″ rectangle. Press the seam allowance toward the colored fabric. Make 4 total, 2 light and 2 dark.

2. Sew the long edges of 2 white 2″ × 9¾″ rectangles to the long edges of each of the units from Step 1. Press the cross arms made with the lighter fabric toward the white and the cross arms made with the darker fabric toward the dark.

3. From the closed end of each cross arm, measure down 6⅜″ on each side and make a small mark. From that marking, cut a 45° angle to create a triangular point in the center. Repeat to make 4.

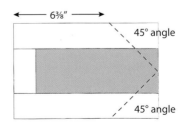

4. Sew 1 light unit and 1 dark unit together, beginning at the point and stopping ¼″ from the interior corner. Press the seam allowances toward the dark fabric. Repeat with the other 2 units.

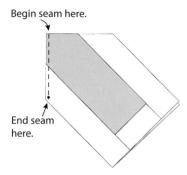

Begin seam here.

End seam here.

5. Layer the units together, nesting the seams. Sew through the center, beginning and ending ¼″ from each corner. Peak at the back and press the seam to whichever side allows all the seams to point in the same direction.

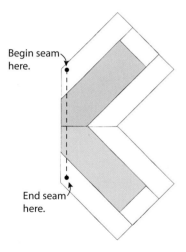

Begin seam here.

End seam here.

6. Place the block right side down. If you pressed the seams toward the dark, you will notice that 3 of the 4 seams point in the same direction, clockwise or counterclockwise. Look at the seams and find the last long seam. Also locate the short seams that are perpendicular to it.

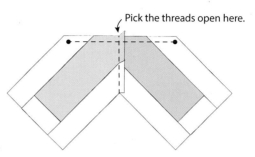

Pick the threads open here.

7. Using a seam ripper or pin, remove the threads above the long seam, on both sides of the four-patch.

8. Looking at the block, see that the seams are now free above the long seam where the points come together. Press the now-open points in the same direction as the short seams.

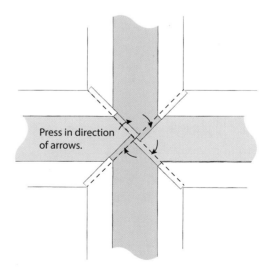

Press in direction of arrows.

Spinning Seams

Opening or spinning the seams is a great way to reduce the bulk where points meet up. I strongly recommend using this technique with the star points after they are sewn into their final locations. The overall method remains the same: Remove the stitches where the points come together on the other side of the long seam. Take the point in your fingers and *very gently* twist the points so that they open up and fall evenly across the intersection. Press open.

9. Determine the bottom point of the cross. Sew a Type 2 border (page 102) with a white 4¼˝ quarter-square triangle. Press the seam allowances toward the dark.

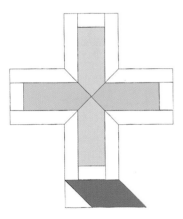

Making the Diamond-in-a-Square Block

1. Sew a white 3⅞˝ half-square triangle to a 4¾˝ × 4¾˝ colored square. Press the seam allowances toward the colored fabric. Repeat with the remaining 3 edges.

2. Add the second round of triangles, sewing a colored 5⅛˝ half-square triangle to each side of the unit from Step 1. Press the seam allowances toward the colored fabric.

3. Add the final round, sewing a white 6⅞˝ half-square triangle to each side of the unit from Step 2. The finished block will measure 12½˝ × 12½˝. Press the seam allowances toward the interior of the block. Make sure there is no shadowing of the darker fabric.

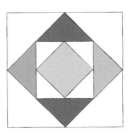

Making the Square-in-a-Square Block

1. Sew white 2″ × 3½″ rectangles to opposite sides of a 3½″ × 3½″ colored square. Press the seam allowances toward the white.

2. Sew white 2″ × 6½″ rectangles to opposite sides of the unit from Step 1 to complete the box around the square. Press the seam allowances toward the white.

3. Sew the long edge of a colored 3½″ × 9½″ rectangle to a side of the unit from Step 2, stopping at a point just over midway through the square. You will finish this seam in Step 5. Press the seam allowances toward the outer rectangle.

Begin seam here. Stop about 2″ from end.

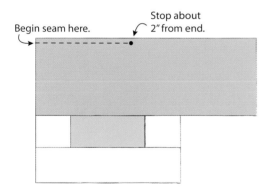

4. Sew the next 3½″ × 9½″ colored rectangle to the 9½″ edge of the rectangle from Step 3. Press the seam allowances toward the outside. Continue with the remaining 3½″ × 9½″ rectangles.

5. To close the first seam, open the first seam and align the edges. Sew it in place, making sure the stitches overlap and lock in the middle. Press the seam allowances toward the outside.

6. Sew a white 3½″ × 12½″ rectangle to the right edge of the block. Press the seam allowances toward the white.

7. Sew a 9½″ × 15½″ white rectangle to the top of the block. Press the seam allowances toward the white.

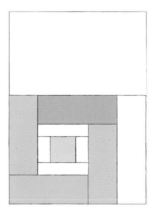

Making the Borders

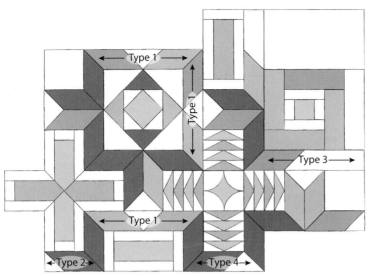

Border types 1–4

TYPE 1: Sew a star arm to a 5½″ quarter-square triangle. Press the seam allowances toward the colored fabric. Sew the second star arm to the other side and press toward the colored fabric. Make 3.

TYPE 2: Sew a 3⅞″ half-square triangle to a star arm. Press the seam allowances toward the colored fabric.

TYPE 3: Sew a 3½″ × 12⅞″ chisel to a star arm. Press the seam allowances toward the colored fabric.

TYPE 4: Sew a 7⅛″ quarter-square triangle to a star arm, beginning on the outside edge as if for the Type 1 border. Stop ¼″ from the point, as shown. Press the seam allowances toward the colored fabric.

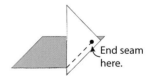

End seam here.

I felt a strong sense of connection between all of us who see beauty and pattern everywhere.

Adding Borders to the Horizontal Rectangle-in-a-Rectangle

1. Sew a Type 1 border to the top of the rectangle block, beginning and ending ¼˝ from the corners.

2. Sew an arm to the left and right edges of the rectangle, beginning at the bottom and stopping ¼˝ from the corners.

3. Finish the corners, sewing the seams from the outer corners and finishing a thread's width away from the previous seamlines. Press the seam allowances to one side.

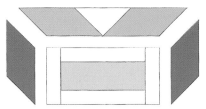

Sew the Type 1 top border first, then sew the star arms to the sides, and then close the mitered corners.

Putting It All Together

Be methodical, take your time, and enjoy the process.

Section 1: Framing the Diamond-in-a-Square

The Diamond-in-a-Square is framed by Star Variation 1 on the left, Star Variation 2 on the bottom, and a Type 1 border at the top and on the right side.

1. Match the points of the borders with the points of the diamonds in the block. Pin everything in place.

2. Beginning and ending ¼˝ from each corner, sew the borders to the Diamond-in-a-Square block. Press the seam allowances toward the outside.

3. Close the mitered corners and press the seams to the side.

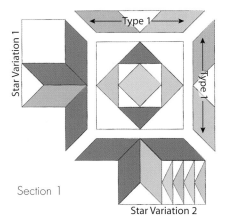

Section 1

Section 2

This section is the previously completed Star Variation 3.

Section 2

Section 3: Square-in-a-Square Block

1. Sew a Type 4 border (arm with chisel) to the bottom edge of the Square-in-a-Square unit.

2. With the 9½″ × 15½″ panel to the left, align the chisel with the right side. Begin sewing from the outer edge and sew to ¼″ from the corner point.

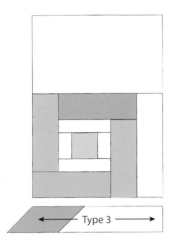

Type 3

Section 4: Bottom Right of Center Panel

1. Sew an arm to the short left edge of the white 6½″ × 15½″ rectangle. Press the seam allowances toward the colored fabric.

2. Align Star Variation 4 so that the Flying Geese are at the bottom left. Sew, beginning from the top and stopping ¼″ from the corner, a thread's width or so from the previous seamline.

3. Sew the miter closed.

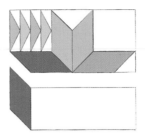

Section 5: Flying Geese and Drunkard's Path

1. Sew together the Drunkards' Path block and the Flying Geese block.

2. Sew on a Type 4 border as shown, beginning and ending ¼″ from either end. Press the seam allowances toward the arm/quarter-square triangle.

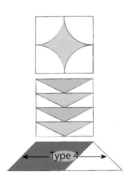

Type 4

Assembling the Left Half of the Panel

1. Arrange the Simple Cross and Section 1 (Diamond-in-a-Square with borders) on your design wall and locate the point where the top of the cross and the left-hand star border join.

2. Pin the top point of the cross with the left side of the star core. Begin the seam at the outer edge and stop ¼″ from the interior corner.

3. Continue sewing the Simple Cross to Section 1, starting and stopping ¼″ from each juncture, until the right arm of the cross has been sewn to the left side of the bottom core.

4. Press all 4 seam allowances to one side.

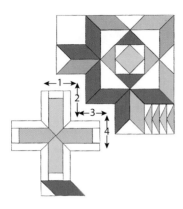

5. Sew a white 6½″ × 9½″ rectangle to the bottom left quadrant of the Simple Cross. Press the seam allowances toward the white panel.

6. Sew a white 6½ × 18½″ rectangle to the left of the cross and star border. Press the seam allowances toward the white panel.

7. Sew the 6½″ × 30½″ panel across the top of the units. Press the seam allowances toward the white panel.

The panel is completed by joining this unit onto the rectangle-in-a-rectangle unit using 3 seams: a long seam to ¼″ from corner, the second seam joining the cross and the rectangle unit, and the third seam closing the mitered corner.

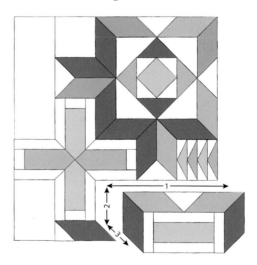

8. Match the white quarter-square triangles on the long edge and pin. Sew from the top, stopping ¼″ from the interior corner.

9. Align the last cross arm with the last border of the rectangle block, shifting the seam allowances and fabric as necessary. Beginning a thread away from the seam in the interior corner, sew to ¼″ from the unfinished corner.

10. Finish by sewing the mitered corner closed.

Finished left half of panel

Assembling the Right Half of the Panel

1. Matching the point where the star arm meets the top of the Square-in-a-Square, sew Sections 2 and 3 together from the top, stopping ¼″ from the interior corner. Press the seam allowances toward the Square-in-a-Square.

2. Finish by sewing the miter closed. Press the seam allowances toward Section 3.

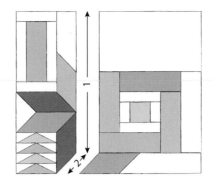

3. Match Sections 4 and 5 so that the right arm of the Flying Geese Cross and the Drunkard's Path center block line up. Sew, starting ¼″ from top and stopping ¼″ from the point of the quarter-square triangle. Press the seams toward Section 4.

4. Sew the miter closed.

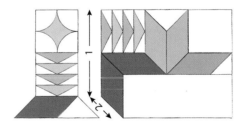

5. Sew Panel 2-3 and Section 4-5 together end to end as shown.

Finished right half of panel

Finishing the Panel

1. Line up the left and right halves, paying particular attention to the points of the quarter-square triangles and the Flying Geese Cross. Pin the pieces in place.

2. Sew the halves together from the top, stopping ¼″ from the bottom corner of the Flying Geese Cross block.

3. Sew the miter closed, beginning from the outer edge and working to the inside corner.

4. Press the seam allowances to the side.

Sew the panels together, long seam first, and then close the mitered seam.

Finishing the Top

1. Sew the white 4½″ × 39½″ rectangle to the right side of the finished panel, long edges together. Press the seam allowances toward the white rectangle.

2. Sew the white 17″ × 58½″ rectangle to the bottom of the panel, long edges together. Press the seam allowances toward the white rectangle.

3. Sew the white 23″ × 58½″ rectangle to the top of the panel. Press the seam allowances toward the white rectangle.

4. Sew the 20½″ × 78½″ panel to left side. Press the seam allowances toward the outside.

Adding the Borders

1. Measure the length of the quilt across the left side, through the middle, and across the right side. Find the average of these numbers.

2. Cut the 2 strips for the inner border to this length. Pin in the middle and at the ends; then pin the remainder of the border, easing the fabric in as necessary.

3. Sew the border and press the seam allowances toward the colored fabric.

4. Measure the width of the quilt top through the top, middle, and bottom and find the average of these numbers. Repeat Steps 2–3.

5. Repeat for the white and blue borders.

6. Layer, baste, quilt, and bind as desired.

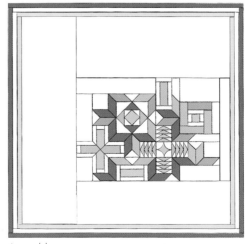

Assembly

Lovely Fishbourne

References and Resources

REFERENCES

Collins, Sally. *Mastering Precision Piecing.* Lafayette, CA: C&T Publishing. 2006.

Hargrave, Harriet, and Carrie Hargrave. *Quilter's Academy, Vols. 1–4.* Lafayette, CA: C&T Publishing. 2009.

Kleiner, Diana E. E. HSAR 252: Roman Architecture. Open Yale Courses. oyc.yale.edu/history-art/hsar-252.

McDowell, Ruth. *Ruth B. McDowell's Piecing Workshop.* Lafayette, CA: C&T Publishing. 2007.

Schamber, Sharon, and Cristy Fincher. *Piece by Piece.* Paducah, KY: American Quilter's Society. 2007.

Walker, George R., and Jim Tolpin. *By Hand and Eye.* Fort Mitchell, KY: Lost Art Press. 2013.

Wolfe, Victoria Findlay. *15 Minutes of Play: Improvisational Quilts.* Lafayette, CA: C&T Publishing. 2012.

Wolfrom, Joen. *Ultimate 3-in-1 Color Tool, 3rd ed.* Lafayette, CA: C&T Publishing. 2011.

RESOURCES

C&T Publishing

ctpub.com

Wash-Away Appliqué Roll (fusible water-soluble foundation paper)

Fishbourne Palace

sussexpast.co.uk > Discover Historic Properties > Fishbourne Roman Palace & Gardens

Roman Way
Fishbourne, West Sussex PO19 3QR
England
Tel: 01243 789829 / 01243 785859

Sharon Schamber

sharonschamber.com

Sharon's Secret Foundation (water-soluble foundation paper)
Also available at purpledaisiesquilting.com

Once upon a time, Amanda was studying for a Ph.D. in classical archaeology. She went as far from home as she could. She studied ancient languages and classical literature and became more than a little obsessed with Homer's *Odyssey*. She studied material culture (the remains of human activity in the archaeological record), art history, and modern ethical questions about how to deal with what was dug up. She excavated in Israel and studied ceramics in Rome, and then she decided to head back to the U.S. and found a job teaching Latin and history at an independent school in New York. There she met and married her best beloved, making a new life—different from her academic one and rewarding in different ways.

It wasn't until a visit with her grandparents in 2002 that Amanda discovered quilting, and even then it was almost accidental. Her decision to leave her Ph.D. program in classical archaeology was fresh, and she felt she had head space to examine other options besides studying.

It was Amanda's Grampa Johnny, in truth, whose love of quilts and textiles influenced her decision to head down to the local quit shop with Gramma that day.

Amanda's grandpa spoke with such love and affection for quilts and the "beautiful clothes back then." Both of her grandparents told stories about all "the kids" (Amanda's parents, aunts, and uncles) making their outdoor gear on the same 1947 Singer machine that was in the guest bedroom where Amanda was staying. All these stories were wildly appealing to her, and she wanted to carry on that legacy of making things with the same machine as the people before her.

Her quilting journey is about all these things: family and traditions, modern and traditional techniques, ancient and contemporary histories, and how we include all these in our craft.

Grampa claimed that this wool quilt, made by his mother in the 1940s, weighed 90 pounds, but it's really more like 25.